S0-EJR-977

The Yellow Suit
A Guide for Women in Leadership

Jacquelyn Gaines

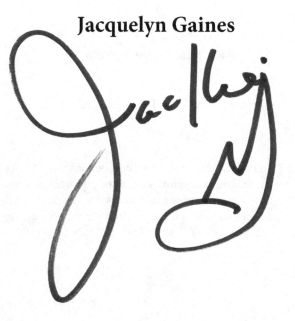

The Yellow Suit: A Guide for Women in Leadership.
Copyright © 2012 by Jacquelyn Gaines.
All Rights Reserved.

Printed in the United States of America. Without limiting the rights under copyright reserved above, no part of this publication may be reproduced, stored in or introduced into a retrieval system, or transmitted, in any form or by any means (electronic, mechanical, photocopying, scanning, recording or otherwise), without the prior written permission of both the copyright owner and the publisher of this book. For information address Arrie Publishing Company LLC., 201 Shannon Oaks Circle Suite 200, Cary N.C. 27511, USA.

Interior Book Design and Layout by
www.integrativeink.com

Library of Congress Cataloging-in-Publication Data

Jacquelyn Gaines.

The Yellow Suit: A Guide for Women in Leadership/Jacquelyn Gaines

p.cm

ISBN-10: 0985050985
ISBN-13: 978-0-9850509-8-6

Printed in the United States of America

10 9 8 7 6 5 4 3 2 1

The scanning, uploading, distribution of this book via the Internet or via any other means without the permission of the publisher is illegal and punishable by law. Please purchase only authorized electronic editions and do not participate in or encourage electronic piracy of copyrightable materials. Your support of the author's rights is appreciated.

Arrie Publishing Company, LLC.

CONTENTS

INTRODUCTION

After more than thirty years in a variety of leadership roles, it is very apparent to me the void in publications on the market that offer women who aspire to be great leaders in business the "rules of the road". *The Yellow Suit's* primary objective is to give women a simple guide that offers tips on how to be a highly effective leader in today's world, despite the fact that the scales of equality are not quite balanced in the workplace.

The book offers the reader the opportunity to explore only those chapters they may find useful or aligns with current challenges they may be experiencing *or* read it from cover to cover. Either way, there is no sugar coating or politically correct discussions. The content includes all those things a great mentor would offer someone who wants to reach their maximum potential. It's what we ladies talk about in private or behind closed doors. And, it's what we need to know to give us an edge in the business world that still tips the advantages toward men.

Even though the book is written primarily for women, I highly encourage men to read it as well. It is important for both genders to understand the mind of the other for true success in the business world, no matter what industry you work in. My experiences have been primarily in health care and through the years I have seen and experienced many of the areas covered in the book. I wish someone had shared some of these tips with me a long time ago. Most of us learned the hard way…after we had failed, fallen on our faces or even lost jobs. It's time for a more proactive approach as we prepare our women leaders for the future!

No matter where you are in your career, you will find a chapter in the book you can relate to and learn from. New and aspiring leaders will find helpful tips on how to begin as a leader, including interviewing for success. For women in their childbearing years, there are chapters on how to successfully re-enter the workforce and on work-life balance. More mature leaders will even find helpful tips for leading throughout menopause. The content areas came from a multitude of conversations with women across the country about what they wanted to know or today's challenges for women in the workplace, especially those in leadership roles. I even got insight from men on their thoughts about women in the workplace and how to succeed. (Remember ladies, we can't just listen to ourselves.)

So, I hope you enjoy the book and find it useful in taking you to the next level of professional and personal growth! I thank all my family, friends and colleagues for their insights and contributions. A special thanks to my husband for standing by me and doing the preliminary editing for this book. Your support is invaluable and precious to me. You give me strength and in return I feel compelled to give some of it back through my work and in books like these.

Much Love,
Jackie

People are like stained-glass windows. They sparkle and shine when the sun is out, but when the darkness sets in; their true beauty is revealed only if there is a light from within.
—Elizabeth Kübler-Ross.

PRELUDE

We all should know that diversity makes for a rich tapestry, and we must understand that all the threads of the tapestry are equal in value no matter what their color."
—Maya Angelou

I remember preparing for the interview like it was yesterday. I pulled out every suit in my closet …black, navy blue, brown tweed, another black one and then my array of beautiful tailored colored suits, pink, baby blue and a muted yellow that I adored. Colors made me feel alive and I was very comfortable with being a woman. The voice in my head from my *Dress for Success* class screamed at me, "black suit, white shirt, black pumps and light jewelry" - the corporate uniform expected of anyone striving to experience the upper stratosphere of leadership. When on earth did this mandate begin? I can guarantee it wasn't from a woman. And, probably came from an era when women first crossed the boundaries into leadership roles primarily held by men. Blending into the leadership culture meant relinquishing femininity for a masculine look and felt equated with power. Even to this day, it continues to be taught at universities all over the country as the preferred interview ensemble as our leaders for tomorrow prepare to enter the workforce, perpetuating the gender bias in corporate America.

On this day, I was preparing for an interview that would advance my career to the next level of leadership, the Chief Executive of a hospital. This was a job held by few women across the country and one I never thought I would be offered in my lifetime. First impressions would be critical for both parties- me as the candidate and for them as the employer. Being the first woman hired to this leadership team meant I had to fit their culture. Moving my family 3000 miles for this job meant this better be a good fit for me as well. As I scanned my options of what to wear, all I could think about was the power of first impressions and the most important element when considering such a huge decision that would impact me professionally and personally. I needed to present as a credible professional and be true to myself. If they want you as their leader, it's not about the color of your suit... but the color of your character and your abilities. So, I went with the yellow suit.

I could stop the story here, but it gets better. On the day of the interview I happen to cross paths with the two other candidates competing for this job. One was a man and one was a woman. It should be no surprise that both wore blue suits, white shirts and black shoes. Oh yeah, the man wore a red tie (surprised?). As the day progressed, the interviews went quite well. I enjoyed the dialogue. There was laughter and a great exchange. I got a good sense of them and I believe they got a good sense of me. Once I returned to my hotel, I got a call from the recruiter who confirmed what I felt, I was a hit! The recruiter went on to say, "The yellow suit took you over the top. The report back to the CEO was that any woman who feels that comfortable with herself to wear a yellow suit to an interview is the kind of leader we want for our hospital." The next day I was offered the job and broke all the *Dress for Success* rules.

Breaking this long standing gender biased dress code will be difficult because women contribute to the madness. We must learn to be comfortable with who we are and not to buy into the belief that women must assume the characteristics of men in order to be effective leaders. In fact, women have innate and learned characteristics that can serve well in today's business environment. **It's time to build a new paradigm that uses the best of both sexes as a determinant of what makes a successful leader**. And, the male dominant world of business will need to listen.

This book will explore the role of gender in leadership and the unique ingredients women add to the achievement of successful outcomes in business. Many of the stories are based on my own experiences as a woman leader in the health care industry for over 30 years and shared by thousands of women throughout the country. Women should feel proud of the attributes they bring to any organization. In addition, women will find many useful tips on how to deal with challenges like work-life balance, rejection and knowing when to leave an organization.

Our touch is unique and doesn't have to be masked or perceived as a sign of weakness. We just need to believe in our own inner strength. We are effective leaders being fully who we are...leading our way.

There are not more than five primary colors (blue, yellow, red, white, and black), yet in combination they produce more hues than can ever been seen. —Author Unknown

WARNING: This book may cause an unexpected *Diversity Growth Spurt*. The subject matter is designed to stimulate your thinking about current realities for women in the workplace. Sometimes, when we pause to see the world through another's lens, the view may not always be comfortable to see. You may even want to run away or deny the images are real. It's only when we leave ourselves open to listen and seek to understand another's journey that real inner growth occurs. That kind of growth can have a powerful impact on our actions tomorrow. So, as you read, if you feel a tug in your gut...you just experienced a growth spurt.

THE EQUALITY FAÇADE

"We ask justice, we ask equality, we ask that all the civil and political rights that belong to citizens of the United States, be guaranteed to us and our daughters forever."
—Susan B. Anthony, Declaration of Rights for Women, July 1876

The ratification of our Constitution's 19th Amendment on August 26, 1920, marked a turning point for America as women were guaranteed the right to vote. Women all over the country celebrated finally being on equal footing under the law with men. Unfortunately, women soon learned that someone forgot to inform men of our newly acquired status and though we have made some strides, real equality is a façade.

Throughout the United States, women earn less, are less likely to own a business, and are more likely to live in poverty than men. Disparities abound regionally and by state, and, even more profoundly, such things as race and ethnicity continue to shape women's economic opportunities. Women continue to earn anywhere from 20-50% less than men for the same jobs held and the higher women go up the food chain, the wider the gap.

Diversity initiatives in many companies continue to play the numbers game to validate their commitment to changing the gender and racial divide, being very proud when one woman or minority is placed at the leadership table of 20 white men. It's celebrated as though the woman has won the lottery for a million dollars. For the woman, she soon learns that the appointment did not denote equality in the job.

Unfortunately, real change must transcend the "number" of women in the top jobs and address the reasons why there are barriers in the first place. Those barriers will continue to prevent the success of even one who has been allowed to join the ranks of their male counterparts.

Attitudes and long standing beliefs about the abilities of women or our "place" in business do not get erased with a number. The number does more to ease the conscious of the oppressor and side step the hard work required to look in the mirror and grow.

I cannot begin to count the number of "firsts" during my career as a health care executive. I was the first minority woman to run a hospital in Oregon, the first minority woman to run the United Way Campaign for the Columbia Willamette and the first minority woman to run a health system in Pennsylvania. I joined the ranks of a handful of minority women in the whole United States to ever hold these jobs. Even though I was proud of these achievements, I knew from past experiences it would not change the challenges I would face based on my race and gender once I crossed the threshold.

I would often tell my colleagues that it took about three to six months post appointment to these very significant roles for folks to get over themselves and beyond my visible attributes of race and gender. No matter how deep my resume or breadth of experience, I would have to prove that I had the same skills assumed to be there in my white male counterparts from day one.

Several employers told me they were "taking a chance on me" even though I was more than qualified for the position (Translation= taking a chance on breaking through the concrete ceiling by adding a woman or person of color to a top job in the organization). Another told me they hoped my differences would be accepted by the "old guard" (Translation= Can a black women be allowed to lead a majority white organization?). Time and patience (mine) usually offer credibility to the hire for some with initial concerns. Others who chose to remain entrenched in their old beliefs and misperceptions never got over themselves.

I guess I could overlook these types of remarks and consider them as statements from ignorant outliers, but the frequency was far too great for that conclusion. This kind of thinking is more the norm than folks would like to admit. And for anyone out there thinking that having a black family in the White House changed this dynamic, think again. At 55 years of age, I still experience the odd looks from others who want to know how I got so far up the food chain. Hard work is still not enough for women and people of color.

I remember being hired as a consultant for a position at a prestigious health system in the mid-west. There was a fairly new CEO and his leadership team that I was scheduled to do a presentation for to enhance their operational performance. The day before I was scheduled to speak, I received a call from the Vice President at the Health System office. He was the primary contact for my consultant work at this location each month. During the call he nervously told me that he had received a call from the hospital CEO who requested that I not talk about my past career role as a CEO during the presentation and he would not be using it in his introduction of me to the group. Just as my mind tried to wrap itself around what I was hearing, the Vice President went on to say it would be okay from me to share my background as a nurse, but not as an executive. Now you have to understand that up to this point, I had limited contact with this CEO or his leadership team. He had not bothered to look at my resume. But, he did know I was a woman of color who had surpassed his level of expertise in the field and he did not want me to share my executive level background with his team.

At this point I could feel my anger rising. It took all my inner strength to maintain a level of professionalism during the call. How absurd! For more than two decades I had successfully led organizations as a President and CEO. Much earlier in my career, I was a clinician, yet he wanted me to discuss a role I had not held since the mid 1990's. Of course, I firmly refused. Why on earth would I wipe out the last twenty years of hard work and achievement to make him feel more comfortable? And, what was the discomfort about…my experience versus his, my gender and /or the fact that I would be the only minority person in a room of 100 leaders. And, by the way…consultants are hired to help leaders grow. If I had no credible background to do the work, why would the System have hired me? Just absurd!

But logic is absent when you try to make sense of situations like the one I just described. Many times the truth may never be revealed for this type of craziness. It's emotional and personal for those involved. It is also imperative that women who find themselves facing this type of challenge hold on to their integrity. Don't compromise. Handled respectfully, you can stand your ground and not lose your job doing it. In this particular situation, I did not make a big fuss about the request.

I did say with conviction that I could not be anything but myself and being a former CEO gave me the tools for the consultant work I offered them to learn from. The CEO never did a formal introduction of me before the lecture, except my name and the organization for which I worked for. I took it upon myself to tell the rest of my story. In an interesting side note- the CEO seemed to be the only person in the room bothered by it and we never spoke of it again. I think he knew he was out of line making such a request. If he made more out of my disobeying him, his superiors could not support his thinking, as it reeked with discrimination. No one would have ever asked him to erase half of his career. In fact, they would have gladly shared it. I know in my heart that being a female, minority and an accomplished executive was at the center of his concerns. How could someone like me teach them a better way...over him?

Diversity is a collective mixture of individuals, cultures and organizational expertise. It is much more than skin color, gender, or background. It's internal and external. Skin color is the result of the level of pigment in our skin; it's a biological event. It doesn't determine how we think, feel, or believe. Gender is random gene selection; we had no choice. It doesn't decide our goals, ambitions, careers or competencies. As children, we learn about morals, values and religious beliefs. But these are relearned, changed or adjusted over the course of our lives. Each of us is diverse in many ways-chosen and random. It is these differences that make each of us unique and commonalities that connect us. So diversity is both visible and invisible...even though the "visible" is what usually provokes the reaction.

For women the reaction continues to be inequality and our journey to those top jobs is filled with potholes and road blocks. Sometimes we even see the clubs of cave men being pulled out of those thousand dollar briefcases.

"Women share with men the need for personal success, even the taste of power, and no longer are we willing to satisfy those needs through the achievements of surrogates, whether husbands, children, or merely role models". —Elizabeth Dole

DNA OR SOCIETY?

*If we are to achieve a richer culture, rich in contrasting values,
we must recognize the whole gamut of human potentialities,
and so weave a less arbitrary social fabric, one in which each
diverse gift will find a fitting place."* —Margaret Mead

The cry is heard outside the hospital delivery room-a baby girl is born into the world. Immediately the social norms are imposed upon this new life as she is wrapped in a pink blanket and nurses tape a small white bow to her hair. Presents abound from family and friends with all the feminine elements only meant for girls. There are no signs of trucks or shades of blue. The imprint that girls require different things is set. The individual wants and desires never come into play as we orchestrate her accepted lifestyle that will follow her long past her birth.

Throughout this little girl's life she will be exposed to a multitude of societal expectations for women and led to believe they are how she should be defined. Any variance from the norm can create tension and challenges in relationships and her experiences with the world. For instance, a preference for jeans and sweatshirts instead of dresses can get one called a tomboy and cause worry for the mom who had been waiting to play dress up. Conversely, a father would quickly deny a male child a doll for fear of him becoming gay, soft or weak.

We even orchestrate the accepted emotions of our children. Aggression in males is celebrated as being tough and tears are unacceptable. In girls, these emotions have a very different meaning. Aggression is unacceptable and tears are seen as just being a girl. These paradigms play out as we grow into adults with the same misperceptions about their meaning for individuals in tow.

Where in the DNA makeup of girls did it say we even like the color pink? And, if we grow to love trucks and race cars, does that place our affinity to our gender in question? And why can't girls be tough and aggressive without cause for concern and boys show a softer side? Some would have you believe that it's our genetic code or even our hormones that push us toward these inclinations including our ability or inability to achieve.

Correspondent Elizabeth Kaledin reports, *in the CBS News Sunday Morning* cover story (March 12, 2005):

> *At a conference on diversity, Harvard University's outspoken president, Lawrence Summers, suggested that intrinsic differences between men and women in the aptitude for science might account for how few women are to be found in the highest ranks of the so-called "hard sciences" -- disciplines such as physics and engineering. The outcry was more than immediate -- it was deafening. MIT biology professor Nancy Hopkins was so offended, she walked out: "When you send this message that maybe it's in your genes, you're asking women every day to prove over and over, 'Yes, I really am good enough to be here.' It's just exhausting."*
>
> *"Somewhere along the road," Barnard President Judith Shapiro commented to Kaledin, "Girls get turned off to science. …If we have stereotypes about what girls can and cannot do, they operate by having girls themselves believe it." Put another way, says Shapiro, sure there's nature -- but don't forget about nurture: "I think we already know so much about the cultural factors and social factors in the way science is organized, that makes it (such) a problem for women, that to start focusing now on innate differences is really a diversion."*

The media plays a big part in perpetuating the norms and roles for women and men through movies, sitcoms and advertisements. Sexism is prevalent throughout them all, accepted because "sex sells". Leaders in any industry are primarily white males even in fantasy. Oprah and Michele Obama are two of the few female giants we can call by name.

These images and their underlying messages become integrated into how we define ourselves and others. They can also limit who we think we can become further accentuating the divide between the sexes.

With regard to intellectual development, The National Institutes of Health (NIH) in Bethesda, Maryland has documented that the size of a male's brain is about 10% larger than that of a female's, however, all proportions are about equal. The larger size was not proven to denote more intellect-so much for the "bigger the better" theory. The research conducted at NIH did show girls and boys differ profoundly in how they hear, how they see, how they respond to stress --and those differences are present at birth. These are not negative attributes, just differences. Society has placed values on them, not our genes.

An article in the New York Times, titled "Hormones, Genes and the Corner Office" by Emily Bazelon (March, 9, 2008) offers additional insight:

> *Women's brains aren't inferior but vary considerably from men's, and this is the primary explanation for the workplace gender divide. Women care more about intrinsic rewards, they have broader interests, they are more service-oriented and they are better at gauging the effect they have on others. They are "wired for empathy." These aren't learned traits; they're the result of genes and hormones. Beginning in utero, men are generally exposed to higher levels of testosterone, driving them to be more competitive, assertive, vengeful and daring. Women, meanwhile, get a regular dose of oxytocin, which helps them read people's emotions, "the truest social enabler."*

Clearly our genes are an important defining factor in our makeup, but do not hold the only key to our future and who we can become. It is my belief that society plays a larger determining role setting the expected norm at our birth. Often those expectations are not in alignment with equality between the sexes or maximizing the potential of our differences. We in turn live up to the expected norm throughout our adult lives, passing on the albatross to our children.

"The woman's movement has created the potential for freeing both women and men from gender straightjackets—myths and preconceptions that encase us in very narrow definitions of what it means to be a male or female in our society. Parents born of a women's movement can foster healthy and happy young men and women free from the inhibiting shackles of gender stereotypes, which ultimately limit all of our human potential." —William S. Pollack, Ph.D. Author of *Real Boys: Rescuing Our Sons from the Myths of Boyhood*

THE MIMIC

Mimic: To assume a resemblance to (some other organism of a totally different nature, or some surrounding object), as a means of protection or advantage.

It's the night before the interview for a top leadership job in your organization. You pick through your wardrobe to find just the right outfit that says "I am a great leader and the one you want for this job!" Your fingers pass by anything with frills or bold colors because you have been through the *dress for success* class that told you that was taboo. Leaders don't dress like that. You finally land on that black suit, white shirt and plain black pumps. As an accent, a small gold chain will adorn your neck replacing the one you love with the colorful pendant. For the interview, you will pull your hair back in a clasp and wear minimal make up. Now you are ready…at least by the rules more than likely created by men.

I cannot believe for a minute that men actually like this look, but in business, especially in top jobs blending into the norm seems to be more acceptable than a person being herself. The norm in top jobs are men dressed in dark suits, white shirts and red ties, thereby driving the attributes of what is deemed "dressing for success". Who said colors or frills equate to weakness or an inability to lead? In a tailored multicolored business suit a woman can confidently assert the skills and gifts she brings to the job. Anyone interviews better when they are comfortable in their own skin, not mimicking who they think they should be.

Maybe it's easier for men to accept women as their peers if we mimic their behavior to a point. And many women buy into this garbage as an ingredient for advancement by stepping right into these shoes, some literally adorning their black or navy suits with neck ties. Women do not need to trade in their own personal style as long as it takes into consideration the professional demeanor of the role, the audience and overall corporate culture (i.e., formal or business casual). It may even prove to uplift the organizational mood that is often depressed, devoid of color and an appreciation for differences.

Colors have always been a trademark defining my spirit as a health care leader. My staff and colleagues used to tell me they always knew if I was raising money or had to speak before a crowd by what I chose to wear. Red always seemed to work in fundraising and when the appearance of power was important. I even started to influence others to wear colors, including some of the most conservative men who traded in their white shirts for muted shades of blue and yellow (Progress can sometimes be slow). My guess is the colors helped, but my persona in the clothes really grabs the attention of the audience I am addressing. I am comfortable in my own skin. Whatever brings that out in a person, male or female, should be their calling card, even if it's that black suit or a very feminine dress. Stepping into the "real you" can be freeing and enhance your effectiveness in any role including the top job. Sure, it may upset the apple cart or challenge the norm, but don't let that stop you. Be confident in your abilities. Ultimately, organizational results, primarily money, is valued more than what you wear.

Mimicking the attitudes of our male counterparts elicits a whole different response than appearance and is usually deemed totally unacceptable for a woman. It can be perceived as threatening to men and even cost you that promotion. Many stereotypes drive what we believe are real gender based characteristics and are reinforced through our social interactions. Men are generally stereotyped to be objective, competitive, logical, independent, aggressive, responsible, rational, and ambitious, whereas stereotypes of women often include characteristics such as being gentle, emotional, intuitive, dependent, sensitive, passive, illogical, nurturing, warm, and accommodating (Dubno, 1985; Eagly & Wood, 1991; Haslett et al., as cited in Dennis & Kunkel 2004). These stereotypes help to illustrate why many think of leaders as being more masculine. A woman leader who is perceived as tough and focused is thought to be unfeminine; one who shows emotion or is perceived as compassionate is criticized for being too soft. The stereotypes of the female role still seem to place women with little to no power and below the stature and capabilities of men.

These societal stereotypes are so strong that many women actually believe them to be true. We allow ourselves to be lulled into a submissive trance that has held us captive for hundreds of years. We feel uncomfortable or torn when we take the risk to break the spell and stand up for ourselves. Some will even attribute failure to an inability to master some of the "masculine" behaviors associated with leadership...saying that it was not a part of their genetic make-up. I say don't believe the hype, believe in yourself.

References:

Dennis, M. R., Kunkel, A. D. (2004). Perceptions of men, women, and CEOs: The effects of gender identity. Social Behavior & Personality, 32, 155-172.

OPERATING IN A WHOLE
DIFFERENT PARADIGM

Your paradigm is so intrinsic to your mental process that you are hardly aware of its existence, until you try to communicate with someone with a different paradigm." —Donella Meadows

As women begin to think about their career journey, rarely do they consider the additional challenges that come with just being female. Our typical day would probably never mirror that of our male counterparts no matter what job we held. There are other roles we need to fulfill that don't have a paycheck attached to them or part of a 5-year career plan.

Here's a typical day for me. Can you identify?

Okay.... 5am--alarm sounds...

Wake up...what a crazy day I have today...Darn, I forgot to pick up the dry cleaning last night...I really wanted to wear that red suit today (power meeting at work)...why couldn't I have just five minutes of quiet time for coffee and the paper...who set up a 7am meeting? Dog barking, husband snoring...who said I was queen of letting the dog out in the morning?

Starbucks on the way in...I really need espresso...three shots please...now I'm wired...at least through the first meeting of the day. Man, I forgot to pull down the chicken for dinner.

Here I am again, the only woman leader at the gathering of white male leadership in our organization. They are all talking about sports and I'm worried about if I will have enough time to do the laundry tonight. Okay, stay with the meeting...be heard... not invisible.

This day is at a very high pace.... office is a revolving door ... fires to put out, emotions to calm, planning underway...my Mom called very distressed about her lab test (my parents are seniors with health challenges 300 miles away). I've always been the caretaker in the family. I have to find time to call her back. Both daughters called...one about anniversary plans and the other with questions about caring for my grandson with a cold. Boss called...needing data. Oh man, its one o'clock...did I eat lunch? I think I have a power bar in my desk. How long has this been here.... it will just have to do.

Next meeting-finance...be assertive, lead, teach...be heard... not invisible. Husband called...yes, I love you and yes I'll be home around 6 and yes I will call the travel agent to get plane tickets for our trip next month and your blue shirt is on the futon in the guest room.

Check e-mails, return phone calls...what on earth will I have with the chicken...man; I have to go to the grocery store for pota-toes. One more meeting...I need to settle this account...I know it won't be pleasant.

Great 5:35...walking out the door...please let me get to the car without being stopped.... thank-you...I made it! Dinner on the table by 7pm...I know my husband's talking to me about something important...so tired...can't keep eyes open.... .... can't think...so tired...

11pm.... why am I downstairs still in my clothes from work... to bed.

Wow...I am a multitasking female machine! Did any of this sound familiar?

For most men this may not ring any bells. But, for millions of women throughout the country...the rituals of our days described previously, are real. We are wives, mothers, teachers, caretakers, re-pairpersons, disciplinarians, housekeepers, chefs and some of us are leaders in business. We are master schedulers and often the nucleus around which an entire family is organized.

And, we women…. we want it all! And isn't that our choice. The numerous roles women assume daily are a part of our make-up and influence how we interact with the workplace. They cannot be separated when talking about diversity or the advancement of women of any ethnicity in leadership.

For women leaders…success in business means we have to find the way to balance all these roles. For example, current societal expectations in the workplace are rarely flexible or accommodating to working moms…. so that forces women to choose. Add in the expectations or norms for people in leadership…like 12-14 hour days…. and this balancing act becomes more challenging.

Even though we would appreciate the considerations of employers in our plight, that organizational change is a long way off. However, there is another way to think about our current conditions while we wait for societal norms to catch up. They could be seen as an advantage. The same skills women have perfected through the years to balance our lives are the same ones that can be used for organizational success. We have so much experience using them that they probably could be incorporated into the header of our resumes.

Think about it. What are the valued attributes in a leader? Integrity, vision, team building, communication skills, technical competency, collaboration and strong people skills are usually at the top of the list. Being a survivor or courageous through controversy and change is also important. Strong leaders are capable of handling a multitude of competing challenges and responsibilities staying focused on the ultimate goals for success.

Now think about the average housewife and mother. Daily maneuvering through the landmines of school schedules, sports practices, shopping, meal planning, bills and chairing the local neighborhood association meeting is second nature. Her toolbox requires a high degree of organizational capacity, technical and financial competency, people and communication skills and the ability to pull her family together to provide the highest quality of life. Notice the consistencies between a successful housewife and how we think about successful leaders? Add in training acquired through education and professional development to that average housewife's toolbox and they could be seen as having an advantage over men who have not incorporated this level of juggling into their repertoire.

And do not underestimate the power of nurturing in moving an entire organization's agenda forward. Nurturing is often defined as *encouraging somebody or something to grow, develop, thrive and be successful*. People will accomplish amazing things when they believe they are valued for their work and encouraged to grow. They are a more energized and engaged workforce. Organizational success becomes the by-product.

The US Department of Labor Statistics (2010) documents less than 8% of jobs are manufacturing/industrial based jobs where employees are valued by what their hands alone can accomplish. Thus, 92% are jobs are about using the employees' intelligence, instincts and ideas to create great outcomes. The human capital no longer resides in just the hands, but now within the head and heart of the workforce. A nurturing leader can unlock that human potential in an organization and take it to a whole different level.

A good example of how nurturing can move even a manufacturing organization to the top is General Motors. They have a long standing history of investing in their workforce incorporating nurturing as a business objective. The program is called "The Employee Enthusiasm Strategy". GM recognizes there is a clear link between investment in human performance and market performance and financial results. In their 2006 Corporate Report GM states:

> *"The investment in our people goes deeper than paying their salaries. GM employees must be equipped with the skills and knowledge required to continuously improve and grow. GM's policy is to educate our workforce to achieve the highest standards. Learning strategy is linked to our business strategy and business goals. Learning enables business performance through the development of mission-critical skills and capability. The business strategy cannot be implemented successfully unless the learning strategy is in place and is effective – upgrading skills and performance globally. Learning is aligned with business results and functional capabilities on a global basis".*

GM offers centralized learning through GM University (GMU), a corporate university established in 1997, and the Technical Education Program.

Another consideration in the power of nurturing is in the retention of our best and brightest. It is a well-documented fact that many talented and productive employees who leave an organization are really leaving a relationship with a leader, manager, supervisor or partner that has gone bad. Therefore maintaining and fostering relationships is a key to successful leadership and should be an attribute that is at the top of any organization's leadership scale. You can't meet financial targets if you have no staff.

Women have been doing this kind of work for years, but their behavior is often devalued because their intentions are misunderstood. A woman who takes the time to talk to an employee about how they are doing or career opportunities, for instance, might simply be considered a nice person--not someone trying to make sure that the staff has enough information to make an important decision. Her business actions become invisible, since the staff attributes her behavior to just being kind. But these interactions are an important retention strategy in major businesses today. They go by different names, such as service excellence and executive coaching.

Women hold the trophy for nurturing in today's world, one of those traits believed to be in our genes. It goes hand in hand with our maternal instinct to care for our young. So being female should serve us well...one would think. Yet, the word nurturing still denotes softness and weakness to many and continues to hold us back in obtaining those top jobs.

Women need to hold their unique attributes in higher regard. Many have bought into the notion than men make better leaders. In a recent MSNBC survey documented in the March 8, 2008 article "Men Rule-at least in workplace attitudes" (MSNBC.com) 41 percent of male respondents said men are more likely to be good leaders, and 33 percent of women agreed. And three out of four women who expressed a preference said they would rather work for a man than a woman.

The survey also identified a boatload of stereotypes among those polled, with many using the optional comment section to label women "moody," "bitchy," "gossipy" and "emotional." The most popular term for woman, used 347 times, was "catty." These comments came from men and *women*.

"One cannot live in a sexist society without absorbing some of those messages, which make women feel worse about themselves and suspicious of other women. The enemy is omnipresent cultural messages, not women themselves." —Janet Lever, Professor of Sociology at California State University

Management is about arranging and telling. Leadership is about nurturing and enhancing. —Thomas J. Peters

References:

Tahmincioglu, Eve, Men Rule –at Least in Workplace attitudes. MSNBC.com/ Business & Careers, March 8, 2007.

THE *SEX* FACTOR

The problem with using sex as the selling point is sex becomes the product being sold. —Heidi Toth

Pick a television show featuring professional women and you will see them clad in low cut blouses or dresses, miniskirts and tons of make-up. Since when do crime scene investigators knee deep in blood and guts needs to use sex as a tool in their toolbox to solve a crime. Did you ever notice the dramatically different appearance contestants for the top job on Donald Trump's show *Apprentice*? Eight women and eight men are challenged to use their intelligence, MBA training and prior experiences to solve complex business problems to impress "the Donald". I guess the eight women thought they needed an extra boost, trading in their business suits for slinky dresses. And the popular show *Sex and the City* might as well come with an instruction manual for how women use sex to advance their professional and social status.

The April cover of *WIRED* magazine (2007) pictured a naked women shielded behind a large corporate document in an attempt to focus on corporate transparency. The inside cover read: "This month features a package of stories about radical transparency, our notion that the next model of business success is laying your company bare to the world—sharing secrets with your rivals, blogging about ideas as you have them, and copping to fumbles and foibles as you make them. The concept was crisp, but we all struggled with how to portray a pretty complex idea in the three-second visual byte metaphor is clear: you're naked." Why not a naked man instead of a woman?

These images continue to support the belief that women who want to succeed in a man's world must use their bodies or womanly ways to accentuate their intellectual talents.

Nina DiSesa, the first woman to become chair of McCann Erickson New York, a global ad agency, actually advises women to use the arts of seduction and manipulation. In her controversial book, "Seducing the Boys Club", she states:

"Manipulation is simply a way to deal effectively with men in our business life and doing it in a way that makes them like us, trust us and promote us. Women tend to forget in the workplace that if a man doesn't like her or trust her, he usually won't back her up. No matter how talented she is."

DiSesa encourages women to use their attributes to their advantage-even crying to manipulate their environment. I beg to differ. I believe women who play by these rules add to the oppressive state of affairs we face each day and fulfill the expectations men already have of women in the workplace. They do nothing to change our future. Is this really the route we want to equality? And, where is self-respect and integrity in this equation?

The experiences of women who use sex and manipulation to advance their careers may not achieve the anticipated outcomes. If they indeed make it to the top job, it may be a short lived victory. Yet some women fall victim to what appears to be the path of least resistance to reach their career or financial goals. They may have all the required education and experience comparable to their male counterparts and choose to fall back on sex as a way to gain the favor of their bosses. This may even be a tool of last resort if the woman has tried unsuccessfully to get ahead just using her brain. Time after time I have seen this play out in the workplace and every time the outcome has not been positive.

I remember on one occasion a Vice President of Operations who feared the wrath of a challenging new President switched gears and used her sexuality to try and gain his favor, retain her job and possibly advance to the role of Chief Operating Officer. She was bright with more than 20 years of experience under her belt. Her advancement to her current role had been slow, but achieved out of hard work and perseverance. Both the President and this Vice President were married.

I watched as she changed her style of dress to be more seductive and used any opportunity to get physically close to our new boss. Rumors ran wild about their secret meetings in darkly lit restaurants and shared hotel rooms at conferences out of town. I watched as the respect employees had for this Vice President reduce to shame and disgust. I watched as she achieved the role of Chief Operating Officer during his tenure, only to be terminated when he no longer held that job. So what was really achieved and what was sacrificed?

In a different organization, a manager I worked with tried the same approach, actually having an open affair with a senior officer however, when the affair went south, his contempt for her was so public she had no choice but to resign.

We all saw the plight of White House Intern, Monica Lewinsky after her affair with President Bill Clinton went public. I am sure the financial rewards came at a very high price. But, can she look herself in the mirror? Will she be a role model for her children?

Why do women feel they need to behave like this, especially women with proven business track records? They should realize the impact their behavior has on themselves, other women and their organization. Men won't take you seriously and women won't respect you. Folks may even start to wonder about why you were hired in the first place and about the values of the employer involved.

Another obvious limitation of using sex to get ahead is that it can have a time limit on its usefulness. Sorry ladies, the "new 50" still looks 50 for most men. A woman's commodity as a sex object typically drops as she ages. There's no longevity in it and anyone who relies on it may actually hurt herself in the long run, since she'll lack the experience and skills to extend her success once her market value as a sex object drops. In this case, maturity is not a virtue in sustaining that top job.

In a front-page story the **Wall Street Journal** cheerily announced, "In Today's Workplace, Women Feel Freer To Be, Well, Women" (2/7/00). This article further illuminates the impact of age and the tools women use to gain an advantage in the workplace. The **Journal** identifies only two roles for women in the workplace: the "stern," "somber," humorless and supposedly asexual women of "about a decade ago" who refuse to trade on their sexuality for success, pitted against the "far more relaxed," "feminine" 20-somethings who are "using the personal tools at their disposal to get ahead professionally"--tools such as Capri pants and tank tops. The article suggests younger women are more inclined to trade in their brain power for the power of sex. Female sexuality is the tool that some think bring men to their knees...but for how long and what happens when they get up? Usually they move on without you. Isn't the evidence in how many women are visible in top jobs today? Less than a handful are CEO's of Fortune 500 companies. Women, get a grip! These tactics are not working. Use your head-the results last longer and you hang on to your dignity.

English Proverb
An idle brain is the devil's workshop.

References:

DiSesa, Nina, "Seducing the Boys Club: Uncensored Tactics from a Woman at the Top", Ballentine Books, 2008.

DOES SIZE REALLY MATTER?

Curvy Woman Anthem: *When you're a plus sized woman, people like to say "yeah, she's cute in the face", as if being full figured is such a disgrace.*

Honey, I'm cute in the face, and I'm thick in the waist. I look good whether I'm in cotton, leather, or lace. I'm beautiful, vibrant and above all, smart. And there's more to me than my weight, I also have a heart. Yes my clothes maybe a bigger size, that just means I have access to a bigger prize. We are all not self-conscious about our weight, and we never have a problem getting a date. So don't think your small frame gives you more pull. I'm a hot, sexy, curvy woman with a figure that's full. —Anonymous

Two candidates apply for the same managerial position in Organization X. If the interview panel had an opportunity to "see" the candidates before one resume was reviewed and asked to choose, what would be there choice? Candidate #1 presents as a middle aged man of medium height with a clearly visible oversized belly hanging over the front of his pants. He is dressed neatly and wears his glasses low on his nose (appearing scholarly). Candidate #2 is an obese woman (an estimated 50-60 pounds overweight) also dressed neatly with mousey brown hair. She has a pleasant look and great smile. With no additional information about their expertise, I believe we all know the answer to this question. The panel chooses Candidate #1.

Obesity continues to be a social liability in the workplace today, but the bias is greater for woman than men. This is especially true with regard to promotions into leadership roles. Overweight men get a pass, with weight gain often seen as a badge that comes with age. Unless the man is morbidly obese, discrimination is unlikely. I cannot say women earn that same badge as they get older. No matter what age, women are expected to remain in "TV image" form and some even get character-istics attributed to them because of their weight that are offensive and inaccurate. In the case of weight and advancing in the workplace for women...*size does matter*!

A study of a group of target applicants for jobs in business by Faulkner (1999) resulted in significantly more negative judgments for obese women than for non-obese women. Participants rated obese ap-plicants as having the following characteristics based only on visual introduction:

- Lacking self-discipline
- Low supervisory potential
- Poor personal hygiene and professional appearance
- Lazy
- Less conscientious
- Less competent
- Sloppy, disagreeable, and emotionally unstable
- Think slower
- Poorer attendance records, and poor role models

These stereotypes could affect wages, promotion, and termination. Research based on earnings of 7000 men and women from the National Longitudinal Survey of Youth indicated that women face a significant wage penalty for obesity and that obese women are much more likely than thin women to hold low-paying jobs (Pagan, J. A., Davila, A., 1997). Another longitudinal study following young adults over 8 years found that overweight women earned over $6000 less than non-obese women (Post, R., 2000). Lower wages were attributed to social bias and discrimination. Obese men were not found to face a similar wage penalty. Obese women received lower promotion recommendations (despite identical qualifications) and were rated to be less accepted by subordinates than the other promotion candidates.

Oftentimes it appears that weight restrictions have been arbitrarily set by employers for certain jobs and not to be found in any employee manual or job descriptions. These restrictions and their accompanying biases are just "understood". Many employers justify their discrimination by saying their organization is going after a certain look and feel and obesity detracts from that goal. The two industries that this is deemed "acceptable" from the general public are in the airline and fitness industries.

Airlines have had great difficulty winning the weight battle in court. Airlines have claimed that weight maximums are necessary for job performance and attendants' health and abilities to perform duties, although physical fitness or actual tests of job-related abilities would be more appropriate standards. Whether it is legal or not, you probably have noticed an increase in the girth of our flight attendants over the last couple of years (an older crowd too). We have become accustom to the slender, well groomed, coiffed flight attendant. If the attendant is significantly larger than the drink cart, we pay attention.

On the fitness front, if we ended up getting an overweight ZUMBA instructor, we may not have the same motivation we get from a slender instructor. If "she" does ZUMBA four-five times a week and looks like that, what hope is there for me? I didn't say it was right; it's just how we are programmed. If an overweight ZUMBA instructor can "shaky, shaky", then what right do I have to judge. Do you think this instructor would ever be promoted to run a regional ZUMBA program or land on a billboard promoting classes in the area? I think not. Unfortunately, s*ize does matter* and I believe women, in this case, are just as guilty of discriminating behavior in and out of the workplace as men. So ladies, check yourself on this one...are you contributing to the madness? With 2/3rds of our society being overweight and 1/3rd considered obese...a major readjustment in our thinking is in order.

This readjustment should begin with our children. Stereotypes about overweight individuals started way before we became an adult. The teasing, hurtful jokes and isolation usually starts very early for an overweight individual and trails them throughout middle school and beyond. Rejection, harassment, and stigmatization of obese children at school is an important social problem. The severity and frequency of this treatment by peers and teachers is disturbing, but, has not been studied fully to understand the entire picture. Mostly what we know is from anecdotal reports or the news. One would expect the side-effects from these early experiences would directly impact one's self-esteem, intellectual self-efficacy, and even where one attends college and seeks employment.

Without a strong support system, the individual can block their own opportunity for advancement just by the way they carry themselves and outward affect. This seems to be more intense for women. Image carries more weight (no pun intended) for women than men, especially in today's world. No matter how many plus-sized ads permeate the print and video media, women hold a mental image of that thin person they want to be. And, these images were ingrained in us before we even hit puberty.

Now, this is not a promotion for obesity. Women definitely should devote more attention to being healthy and fit. This is a definite area of opportunity for many. The plight of obesity in this country is real. But women come in all shapes and sizes. Except for the rare cases in which excess weight makes it impossible for a person to perform a job, overweight individuals deserve the same access to employment possibilities as do thin people and deserve to earn as much for their work. All big-boned women are not un-healthy and a risk for employers. *Size should not be used as an immediate indicator of capability to do a job or to be a leader.* This type of thinking is totally unacceptable.

The Napoleon Complex

Short men and tall women…sometimes seen as a lethal combination in the world of business. This is especially true in a variety of combinations- if the woman reports to the man, the man reports to the woman, peer to peer and in competitive situations for the next job on the career ladder. Although not as widely discussed as obesity, a woman who towers over a man in the workplace can often evoke feelings of insecurity and mistrust in her male counterpart. She can further find herself a victim of unfair treatment, the etiology not even understood by the deliverer. This phenomenon is often called the Napoleon Complex. The name comes from a theory that short statured men like Napoleon Bonaparte (5 ft. 2) and Joseph Stalin (5 ft. 4), both dictators and tyrants, demonstrated angry and aggressive behaviors in an attempt to overcompensate for their height.

Overcompensation is one of the ego defense mechanisms as described by Freud, the idea being that the individual could this way protect themselves from the belief that they were smaller in size. At the same time the lack of confidence regarding their height might cause them to try and distract from it by proving themselves able to "mix with the big boys". This overcompensation can sometimes lead to height discrimination in the workplace.

At first blush, the concept of real height discrimination is almost laughable. After all, we don't typically think of height when we discuss types of discrimination. Yet there is no denying that we place a high premium on height, be it social, sexual, or economic, and our preference for height pervades almost every aspect of our lives. But the rules for height are situational. In models, height is treasured and perceived as an asset to their careers. In this case short females who want to model are the ones on the discriminatory end of the stick. Skill is irrelevant. This is seen in basketball with short men versus tall men. This time tall men prevail.

But in business, tall women are fine, as long as they are not directly working with men substantially shorter than themselves. Usually, the problem is not from the woman, but from the man who just cannot get pass the age old stigma that comes with being height challenged. Again, this is not about skill, but stereotypes and misperceptions. Men of short stature already experience the prejudice that emanates from their own gender. There is long-standing public opinion about height and the ability to lead. Think of our choices for President. Name a short President...except for our forefathers when all men were short. President Lincoln broke the mold.

One business expert has suggested that an additional four inches in height "makes much more difference in terms of success in a business career than any paper qualifications you have" and that it would be better to be "5 ft. 10 and a graduate of N.Y.U.'s business school than 5 ft. 6 and a Harvard Business School graduate." (Harbison, Georgia, 1990) Another commentator concluded that "being short is probably as much, or more, of a handicap to corporate success as being a woman or an African American." They go on to state that "it is hardly a co-incidence that 58 percent of Fortune 500 CEOs are six feet or taller (compared with roughly 14.5 percent of all men) and 30 percent are 6'2" or taller" (Jones, Del, 2008). The thing to note from both of these sources is that they are talking about men, not tall women.

This whole theory about how short men feel about close working relationships with tall women is often fodder for women in powder rooms and female only gatherings across the country. But jokes and lighthearted stories don't erase the pain or workplace discomfort that accompanies these events. Many women feel that their skills or ac-complishments are often downplayed so as not to be more than their shorter statured bosses. Some even have experienced humiliation that comes in the form of statements from their boss or even shorter male peers that demean them in front of staff as a way of keeping them in their place.

Even if the same degree of research validation does not exist on this topic as with other forms of discrimination, tall women most certainly have felt the wrath or ill will of short men in the workplace. Just to be fair, this theory does not apply to all short men…but more than a handful is too many. There is also little or no discussion about height as the underlying cause of the discourse. It's one of our more silent forms of discrimination where **size does matter**.

What's interesting about the relationship between tall women and shorter men is what appears to be a reversing trend in personal or dating relationships. In the court of public opinion, tall women who are in relationships with shorter men are now accepted. Even the discussion about height differences is more open than in busi-ness. The media prominently shows tall women with shorter men on the red carpet in a positive light. The snickering about stars like Tom Cruise needing heals has diminished. On the dating scene, be-ing a short statured male is not a liability in the public eye. I am not convinced that this would hold true for most ladies behind closed doors. I think we still like a tall glass of water.

Big Wallet/Little Wallet:
What if You Make More Money Than Your Man?

Another sensitive area where size does matter is when the woman makes more money than the man. This may be less an issue today than it was even a decade ago as values of old fade with the new generation of "Xers" replacing the "Boomers" in the workplace. But, the imbalance of who's the breadwinner is still a source of relationship problems on the home front for many. This challenge may escalate for women in leadership roles, because there may be an imbalance financially *and* with the woman carrying the title of leader (denoting an imbalance in perceived status and power if her mate does not have a job of equal status).

When a woman makes more money than a man, it can result in the man feeling emasculated and insecure (and therefore, unhappy and unfulfilled in the relationship). A man's self-worth and value is linked with his ability to provide for his woman and family, and be successful in his career. So when a woman makes more than a man, he may feel he isn't as valuable and needed to his woman. He may then feel unhappy in the relationship and begin to look elsewhere toward a relationship where he can feel more like the provider and more needed, as a man.

The key is to always keep talking and look at *all* contributions to the relationship, not just the obvious financial contributions. There is no written rule that the man needs to make the most money. This is an old value that needs to fade. *Wallet size should not matter* (unless it's completely empty). Men can stay home with the children and not lose their masculinity. No matter how far we think we have come, we still have some cultural growth in this area.

Ladies, if you make more money than your man and your job status is at a higher level…be sensitive to the impact this may have on the male psyche. He may need a boost to his male ego. Allow him to give advice, fix things around the house, kill some bugs, change your oil, open doors for you and protect you. If you shun his masculine efforts in all areas, he'll feel like he has nothing to offer you. Make him feel like a man as you take a more traditional feminine role in areas other than money.

The question often arises, "well wouldn't YOU rather have your son be 6'2" than 5' 4"? I suppose. His life would be ten times easier as long as we continue to worship tall stature. However, I would rather see a more enlightened culture in which it didn't matter so much. I'd like to think we've made some progress since the Stone Age.
—Maxwell Smart from The Pop Culture Information Society

References:

Falkner, N. H., French, S. A., Jeffery, R. W., Neumark-Sztainer, D., Sherwood, N. E., Morton, N. (1999) Mistreatment due to weight: prevalence and sources of perceived mistreatment in women and men. Obes Res 7: 572–576.

Harbison, Georgia, *A Chance to Be Taller*, TIME, Jan. 8, 1990.

Jones, Del, *The Bald Truth About CEOs: Executives Say They'd Rather Have No Hair Than Be Short*, USA TODAY, Mar. 14, 2008

Pagan, J. A., Davila, A. (1997) Obesity, occupational attainment, and earnings. Soc Sci Quart **78**: 756–770.

Post, R. (2000) Brennan Center Symposium Lecture. Prejudicial appearances: the logic of American anti-discrimination. California Law Rev **88**: 1–40.

SINGLE LADIES

"Being single used to mean that nobody wanted you. Now it means you're pretty sexy and you're taking your time deciding how you want your life to be and who you want to spend it with."
—Sex and the City

With the increase in divorce rates and women staying single longer, there is a greater likelihood that if a woman is hired into a leadership position…she may be single. The traditional view of leaders having a spouse and children may be fading from current realities. I would venture to say that single ladies may even have an edge for these top jobs, over their married sisters.

Married women typically have moved into leadership when their family responsibilities at home have stabilized…the kids have gone off to school and some of the stressors that go along with having young children at home go with them. Single women may have other life challenges, as well, but do not seem to attract the same degree of focus as the married woman. Employers worry about the reliability and flexibility required in leadership. What if they get pregnant, or have a sick child or a family crisis? The employer often assumes that the married woman will make a choice for family regardless of the impact on the workplace and that the single woman will choose work. These unspoken variables may offer single ladies an edge.

Now, if you are a single mom, you may lose that edge completely because of the cultural biases inherent in that role as well. If you add race or ethnicity into the equation, the chances for career advancement is further compromised. I periodically hold seminars on diversity in the workplace for leadership groups around the country. There is a table exercise I conduct which asks participants to choose from a group of candidates for leadership roles with their organization. They are to share their best fit candidate based only on the description offered and why they didn't choose the others. The only information about the candidates is listed below. Guess which candidates did not get selected?

- A morbidly obese female with her graduate degree
- A homeless man recently separated from his wife with three kids
- A 60 year old white male with his bachelor's degree
- A single Latino female with one child
- An Asian man running his own nail salon

Overwhelmingly, the vote goes to the 60 year old white male and the Asian man running his own nail salon. These results have been repeated no matter what leadership group or where they are located in the country. Participants saw the older man having maturity for the job and more acceptable for leadership based on organizational norms to hire white males into leadership. (I was shocked by this degree of honesty as well.) They saw the Asian man having the business savvy, even though there was no mention of whether the salon was successful or not. Success was presumed. And, participants were emphatic about ***not*** hiring the single Latino female with one child for the mere fact that she could not live up to the responsibilities of leadership. Wow! This is without any other knowledge about the woman. These stereotypes are real and color the minds of potential employers.

Women enter the workforce and leadership roles at different points in their life cycle. Different than our male counterparts, we are often judged or valued as a reflection of that part of our journey. The truth is that it should not determine our ability to lead. How we manage these different stops along the way- single, married, with children, graduate education…is ours to manage. The employer can and should be sensitive to the varied needs of women, but not judge their success on an unexplored variable.

Being single does not automatically mean you have nothing going on in your life or that you can commit to long hours and complete devotion to your job. Just as being married or a mother does not mean you will be distracted. We all have competing life priorities…even men! It's how we balance them to achieve success in both parts of our life- work and personal- that is a foundation for success as a leader. In addition, a diverse workplace made up of people at all the various stages of life, offers an organization depth of vision and ideas. Uniformity is boring.

"You have brains in your head. You have feet in your shoes. You can steer yourself in any direction you choose. You're on your own. And you know what you know. You are the person who'll decide where to go." —Dr. Seuss

THE FALSE SISTERHOOD

My Sorority Sisters (can substitute Greek name in title - like "My Phi Mu Sisters")

There's one to help you when you're hurting and another who's always there to have a good time.

There is one who will pray for you, and one who will cry with you.

Some will fight for you, and others who will put you in your place when you're out of line and need a reminder.

There is one who understands your roommate issues or your family problems.

There is one who will sympathize with you and another who confronts you with all your faults, but every one of them love you - because they are your sisters.

Here I am two whole months as the newly appointed CEO for an area hospital. I am also the first minority female to hold this post in this organization's entire history. I know I will be under a microscope for a while. Every decision I make will be scrutinized and questioned. This will especially be the case with new leadership positions that become vacant. My chair wasn't even warm before I got a visit from a young black woman I had never met. She was currently in middle management, desiring a role in executive leadership. The encounter went something like this:

"Ms. Gaines, my name is Sharon and I have worked for this health system for five years. I can't tell you how you are the talk of the health system! All your sisters here are so glad this system finally hired a black woman to a CEO post. Now we all have a chance."

First of all, I didn't think I had any sisters in this state, but I knew she was referring to my race. Secondly, my radar went up on the assumption that because I was black that I would automatically promote other black women without consideration of expertise and fit for whatever role they desired. I love mentoring others, but I was not sure this is what Sharon had in mind. The conversation continues:

"Ms. Gaines, I know you have an open Chief Operating Officer position and I really hoped you could hook a sister up. I am sure you know the struggles of being black in primarily white leadership structure. You can't get ahead. I have paid my dues and deserve this promotion."

There was never any review of skills or resume in the fifteen minutes I listened to Sharon's views on what commitment to the "sisterhood" meant. She wanted me to give her the job because she presumed sharing the same race gave her certain rights. When she discovered I had a different point of view, she denounced me as a real *sister.* I had, in an instant, become "one of them" and stripped of my *sister* title. Now, I not only had to prove myself to the all-white leaders who hired me, but to the league of *sisters* who were watching me as well.

Why do we do this to each other? Why do we believe that if we belong to a certain group (it doesn't even have to be race), that affords us special privileges or gifts without working for it? This statement does not mean I believe in dismantling affirmative action. Or that you should not mentor others you do have a strong affiliation with to succeed or achieve deserving leadership role. What I am talking about are women engaging in the same games we detest from men like "the boys club" and dressing it up and calling it "the sisterhood". In business that translates to men hiring other men that walk, talk and act like them. We did not get to the racial imbalance in leadership without "the boys club" playing an active role. Ladies, we do not have to add to this madness.

Webster defines sisterhood as:

1. The state or relationship of being a sister or sisters.
2. The quality of being sisterly.
3. A society, especially a religious society, of women.
4. Association or unification of women in a common cause.

No where do you see any reference to what we owe to our sisters for such an affiliation.

Sororities are a great example of what true sisterhood means. Their longevity since the mid-1800s demonstrates the power of "the sisterhood". They primarily grew out of the need for women to band together when women were first allowed admission to all male universities. Currently the largest non-cultural sorority is Chi Omega with 17,000 collegiate members at any given time. Delta Zeta is the second largest and Alpha Phi follows in third. There is even a world-wide organization called **Circle of Sisterhood**, whose mission is to leverage the collective wisdom and influence of sorority women to support entities around the world that remove educational barriers for girls and women, uplifting them from poverty and oppression. Another organization, called **The Color of Sisterhood** seeks to place value upon humanity through unity and alliance. Wow! Now that's a lot of woman power.

Most sororities are anchored in a common goal of helping their members better themselves in a social setting. They can be specifically organized for service to the community, for professional advancement, or for scholastic achievement. Many sororities reach beyond their own group to support others in a variety of philanthropic initiatives. Early sororities were highly competitive in nature, considered by some to drive divisiveness on college campuses. Even though some of that exist today, there is more emphasis on more noble community contributions like fundraising and preparing our leaders of tomorrow. Sporting events and "step" battles have replaced the fierce competition between sororities seen in the past.

Sororities are not without internal challenges. Hazing rituals and other initiation ceremonies still exist and cause controversy for college campuses, though they are not as prevalent today. I am sure many of us have memories of rituals of the initiation requirements of joining a local sorority. For me, it was the Alpha's in Maryland. I can never forget the public humiliation of crawling through a local mall with a dozen other girls, a pacifier in my mouth, being yelled at by a fully credentialed Alpha. That experience was only topped by standing outside in a bathing suit being pummeled by tomatoes, slime and raw eggs. I still can't figure out how that made me a better contributor to the Alpha sisterhood, but it was a rite of passage into this sisterhood.

Barring these side notes to sororities, their underlying values could be emulated in the world of business. The operative words to remember:

- Unified for a common cause
- Support for scholastic and professional achievement
- Community service

We Have Been Given a Wonderful Gift

We have been given the chance to experience the wonders of life together.

The good times I treasure the most, and some of the best memories I have, were spent with you. In the worst times, we only became stronger.

I want you to know that in difficult times I will not stand behind you or walk in front of you, I will walk beside you, and I will always be there.

No distance or person can take away what we have or who we are, because you are my sister... always.
—Gwendolyn Moore

This kind of bond with other women, no matter what race, in a business setting can be powerful and should be encouraged. It doesn't mean we are setting up a male versus female workplace. It means, woman understand the needs and challenges of other women and are in the best position to advise, teach and nurture growth and development. It does not mean, because we are "sisters", we are obliged to give a fellow sister jobs or advancement, not deserved or earned.

One of the smartest women I know in the health care industry gave me such a chance. Jane had watched my career, offered me personal counsel and opened a door to advancement because my skills and experience seemed a best fit for that organization. She pushed me to grow in ways I didn't even know I could. Today, when I look back at that experience, I am proud of myself. I am also grateful that she did not "give" me the job because of our affiliation through a local leadership organization. I am grateful for her mentorship, because I was able to take my lessons learned and go even further in my career because of her support of me. Today, we are still good friends and cherish our relationship. Jane continues to support other women in their quest for leadership in health care and I work hard to be like "Jane". By the way, Jane is a white health care executive…one of finest ever to lead a hospital in Maryland. She continues to achieve numerous awards and recognition for her work and has a strong sense of community responsibility. She faced many personal and professional challenges along the way, but her inner strength and spiritual base kept her focused and highly effective. I consider Jane a *"sister"* in a world that continues to be dominated by white males. My respect for her is exponential.

My *sisters*, do seek the mentorship you need to get you ahead. We are out there and willing to help you grow. Strengthen your resume. Take classes you need to advance to the next rung on your career ladder. Learn from others willing to show you new skills and the tools of your trade. Yes, for women, the road is harder and you will encounter glass and concrete ceilings. But, don't use the illusion of "sisterhood" as your stepping stone to success.

> *These are the women who have shown me kindness and given me strength. They give me refuge when I am afraid and support me for who I am. They both believe in me, and challenge me to change. But most importantly they are the inspiration for the person I am becoming.* —Jackie

FEMALE GUILT

It's easier talking to a wall, because a wall doesn't walk away, doesn't push me away, and certainly doesn't make me feel like shit. —Lizzette Olguin

After a long day at work, you drag your tired mind and body across the threshold to your home, and enter the world where family should be front and center. All day long you have been "talking, talking, talking". The last thing you desire is more talking. If you have children, they are meeting you at the door, anxiously awaiting your attention. You are quietly thinking, somebody...anybody...help me. The whole drive home, all you could think about was a long hot bath, a glass of wine and maybe your husband would be up for a back rub. But as soon as you open the garage, you are snapped back into the reality of dinner, housework, elementary school projects and a husband who demands as much attention as the kids. What made me think I could manage being a leader, working incredible hours *and* be a good wife and mother? If this describes you...welcome to *female leader guilt.*

"Honey, why can't you listen to me", says your husband. "Family is never first for you and what's happening to us? This job is killing our relationship." These sharp statements just compile the guilt you are already feeling. Then why don't you stop, throw in the career towel and just be the wife and mother everyone wants. Most of the time you want it too (even though you are happy you have a job when the kids are out of control or you have a fight with your husband). You don't throw in the towel because you actually enjoy the role of a leader and all the prestige and recognition that comes with it. And, you worked hard to get there. So guilt takes over as you try and reconcile the challenges of balancing both your desires in your head and heart.

I am certain that your husband did not have one thought about dinner (except eating it), housework or taking care of the kid's needs while he opened that garage on his return home from work. But he may have been thinking about what the night might hold for him in your bed. He probably had thoughts about the cold beer in the refrigerator, sitting in his favorite chair and hoping the kids would be quiet enough to let him take a nap before dinner. If he had a special room or man cave that was just for him, he would probably escape there, not looking back until you called him to eat. He too had a rough day at work and all he can think about is relaxation and recuperation. It's hard managing that plant...all the complaints daily and demands if you're the boss. No **man leader guilt** to be found. Sound familiar?

And don't even start talking about sexual desire. I don't imagine it's at the top of a working woman's list of things to do when they arrive home. If given a chance to decompress...maybe. There's even female guilt around sex or said better, lack thereof. This does not mean that work causes our sexual desire to freeze. The real deal is that we are "damn tired" and there doesn't appear to be relief or even an understanding that we need an escape hatch like men. Other duties call our name. We need a "woman cave"!

The tension between a spouse/partner and the working woman can intensify without discussion and attention to the relationship. Multiply the tension and the guilt if the working woman holds a significant leadership role. So, does this tension account for a larger divorce rate among working women? Past research would lead us down this path. However, in present time, it appears as if the sands are shifting. This could be the result of an ever increasing number of women in the workplace. Maybe more couples are trying to figure out how to accommodate a more balanced approach on the home front out of economic necessity.

Marriage has some implicit cultural norms. The concept of marriage carries a few assumptions including a monogamous relationship, co-residence, and a long-term commitment between a man and a woman who typically have children together. Divorce is the separation of such an arrangement. Economic factors and satisfaction with the married relationship are considered the two most important factors influencing divorce.

A current study by Sayer and England (2011) documented the impact of the rising incidence of women in employment and other factors on divorce. It followed married couples from 1987 till 1994 and found that just being employed did not influence divorce. The study found that women's employment did not encourage them to exit from marriage if they were satisfied with their marriage. For those who assessed their marriages negatively, being employed raised the odds of leaving. The study also found that wives' employment had no effect either positive or negative, on men's initiation of divorce. However, men's employment encouraged women to stay in the marriage.

Translation= Ladies, focus on your relationships and never stop talking to your partners. Even through rough days, find a time to find solace in each other. There is some truth in the old saying, "never go to bed angry with your partner". But, if your relationship was lousy before the job, don't expect miracles after you start working or step into those leader shoes. The job itself may not be the cause of your discourse, but it may take you over the top.

The guilt women feel goes back to a different time in history. A time when there was a societal expectation that women stay home and care of the home, their spouses and children. If they did have a job, there came a time when the woman was expected to leave the job to assume her rightful place at home. Even though that era has passed, the script still plays *in our mind*. It's what we observed with our parents and it's what we believe our family and friends say behind our back. "She should really be home with those kids and not so wrapped up in that job."

This script comes with feelings of abandonment, depression and that we are being judged as less than competent in our personal responsibilities. However, times have changed and we need to write a new script where there is not just one option for women who chose to work or be a leader in business. And women need to come to grips with their guilt. How much of what we feel is reality or perceptions that haunt us from another time in history? Because we work, are our children really worse off? Research has already shown us that relationships are already beginning to shift based on the fact that today two parent working families are the norm. Male roles are being re-defined every day.

When looking at alternatives, women should look at the quality of the time they do have with those closest to them and not just the quantity of time. I am positive, thirty minutes of focused, uninterrupted time with your husband or taking that same time to read a book with your child will be more memorable than the 30 minutes you were not at home due to work.

So, now what do we do?

We may not be able to erase all the guilt we feel, but we can try to find peace with the choices we have made. Have a good mental conversation with yourself. Get out a pencil and paper and **write down the reasons you work.**

We all work for different reasons. We love our jobs. We need the money. We don't want to risk dropping out of a competitive field when new positions are scarce. We realize we'd be miserable as stay-at-home moms and would make our children unhappy. We want to set an example of a successful, independent wage-earner. We love to lead!

Write down your own motivations. Once you've reassured yourself that you're doing what you need to do, then simply let go of the guilt. Trust yourself and the choices you've made for your family.

But keep the list. When guilt arises again – and it will – pull it out to refresh your memory.

Play hooky from time to time. Oftentimes, leaders push themselves so hard they forget to take time off even for a vacation. This seems especially true for women leaders. We usually have more than enough vacation time, but we worry what we will miss and sometimes what will happen in our absence. And, we hardly ever consider time off longer than a week. But, we all need time to refresh and renew. We actually are better leaders when we take the time to breathe and reconnect with our family and friends. Escape with your significant other for an erotic play date, play in the back yard with your children, take a girl trip with your best friend, spend quality time with your parents...

allow that other side of you to be free of the daily grind of work, no matter how much you love your job. Make playing hooky an event on your calendar with as much importance as that business meeting with your boss.

If you are a working Mom, **acknowledge the loss** you may feel leaving your children each day for work. Remember, no Mom will be able to witness all the wonderful things our children will do and experience in a day. But we can make the times we do share special. I remember how much I mourned not being there when one of my children took their first steps. Even though she was with her Grandmother, I felt I should have been there. I should have been the one crying when it happened and laughing with joy. Nothing at work could match that experience. But, I wasn't there.

It's okay to be sad about missing those precious moments while you chase your professional dreams. There is no magic pill or advice I can tell you to change the outcome, unless you make a choice to walk away from your career. However, if you dwell on the sadness, it will eat you alive. Mourn the loss and accept that this is part of your life's journey. There are always tradeoffs for our choices. But, we can make the most of what we do experience with our children. Pay sound attention to balance and teach that to your children as well.

Keep the communication channels open to those who love and support you. This is often the hardest thing to do, but the most important. Many female leaders keep their thoughts of guilt or inadequacies as a wife, partner or mother to themselves. They don't want to admit that their choices may not have been the right choices at this time in their lives. They may want to stop or make a change, but feel it would mean they have failed. Certainly, other women have managed…at least it seems. Little do they know that those "other women" who appear to have it all together are probably having very similar thoughts and challenges behind closed doors. We all wear a mask for the public eye. Beware of thinking that the other couple seems to have it all. They both work, have great jobs and their kids appear happy. What's wrong with me? Why do I have all this guilt?

Communication and letting out those feeling with a friend or your spouse/partner is an imperative for your mental health. As my husband often tells me, "I can't read your mind. If I knew what you were thinking, maybe I could help. Let me in sometimes. You are not in this alone." But we don't. We women have convinced ourselves that if we talk, we may have to make a decision to give up on our career and be relegated to only the role of wife and mother. Some women want more. We never think there may be a place in the middle. Maybe the housework could be split. Maybe you could work a 36 hour week instead of a 40 hour week. Maybe it's time to hit the pause button for a year and get your home life in order. The possibilities are endless. We will never know if we don't talk. Guilt could be replaced with a plan. It may not resolve all your feelings, but it could take the edge off.

A wounded conscious is harder to heal than a wounded heart.
—Jose B. Cabajar

References:

Sayer, Liana; England, Paula; American Journal of Sociology (May 2011); *She Left, He Left: How Employment Affects Women and Men's Decisions to Leave Marriages;* Palo Alto, California.

FROM THE MALE PERSPECTIVE

Men are clinging to football on a level we aren't even aware of. For centuries, we ruled everything, and now, in the last ten minutes, there are all these incursions by women. It's our Alamo. —Tony Kornheiser

To check-in on current views of men about women in the workplace and specifically women leaders, I asked men from diverse business backgrounds to answer a few questions. Though not a formal research study, it does offer a qualitative snapshot into the male mind. Many of their responses are outlined below and may surprise you or give you hope for a better future for us ladies. I asked each participant to give honest and not just politically correct answers. (My husband tells me, however, that some men may not be so inclined to reveal their "real thoughts" especially regarding women. So add that to the soup when thinking about the responses.) All chose to remain anonymous (interesting, huh?).

What has been your experience working with a female boss (advantages and disadvantages)? And, would this be a desired relationship in future employment?

- I've had great experiences with two female bosses for the majority of my 26 years in healthcare. I worked with the first for approximately seven years and she greatly influenced my abilities as a clinician during the first half of my career. Likewise, the second was most instrumental in mentoring my growth and development as a leader for the better part of 13 years and counting! I find female bosses tend to recognize and model the importance of work/life balance more consistently than men particularly when the scope of leadership responsibilities increases over time. Often, female bosses are still primary caretakers within the home and of extended family members and must maintain balance between personal and professional demands out of sheer necessity. The result is someone who tends to have greater capacity for being empathic of others (peers, subordinates, colleagues, etc.) in similar workplace situations as compared to their male counterparts.

- I've worked with several female bosses over the years. Some are exceptional leaders and some have struggled with leadership. This has been the same as when I've worked for a male boss. To me it comes down to being competent with your skills and your ability to listen and lead. You don't have to use the power of a position or title instead of developing your interpersonal skills and being a great communicator that makes a good leader.

- I have worked for two female bosses in my lifetime. My experience is that female bosses are sticklers for details and want the job duties performed as near to perfect as possible. The desire for perfection can make them real bitches. They tend to hold a grudge or even lash out at employees that they deem to be falling short of their expectations. The positive to this is that females do seem to do a more efficient job then MOST males. The negative is that they can squash some employees drive and energy towards their position. I would prefer to always have a male boss. Males are a lot more relaxed as bosses and only care that that job gets done correctly, not necessarily perfectly.

- I have worked for terrific women bosses and miserable male bosses. I have also worked for terrific male bosses and miserable women bosses. From my perspective, there are no particular advantages or disadvantages as a function of gender. I am interested in someone who can help me put my particular strengths and talents to good use and then get out of the way and let me do my job without micromanaging me.

- My experience with female bosses has been mostly positive. The positives: (1) more family oriented (2) more approachable (3) more sensitive to minority needs (sex/ race/ disabilities) (4) more nurturing environment. The negatives: (1) more emotional (2) seem to not buck the system/ not risk takers (3) moodier. Having been a manager for many years, I really have no preference as to the sex of my immediate director. I have seen examples where female managers have made more favorable decisions for other female employees. Example: During one push to promote females, females with little or no experience were hired over males, because the females had the "potential" to succeed.

- In general female bosses tend to be a little more emotional/ caring if there is a family matter and in general seem to empathize more. They seem to be a little moodier. Personalities tend to vary from day to day. Whereas, male bosses are either consistently a nice guy or a jerk.

- I've worked with three female bosses, and each experience was quite different. But, never experienced any major problems. Please understand, I grew up in a single parent (mother) environment along with two older sisters that became surrogate parents. Because of this, I can't stand to be around women that expect men to do everything for them. I like strong women that take charge and don't need a man to tell them what to do.

Advantages of female bosses/leaders:

- Thinks beyond the job
- Cares about people
- More sensitive and "soft skills" conscious
- More process oriented

- More willing to accept an employee's weakness
- Strong Leaders
- Hard workers.....more so than men
- Better Teamwork
- Better communicators
- Better at multitasking

Disadvantages
- Can be too emotional
- Less results oriented
- Less versed/comfortable with financial matters
- Become overwhelmed with tasks.....men tend to break it down into workable components
-More likely to value loyalty over competency and performance
- Play favoritism (men do this as well)
- Get caught up in office antics
- Over extenuate with others that they're in charge. If you've got the title, smarts, savvy, confidence, and leadership ability than you won't have to impose your authority.

What are your views about women who work when they have children at home?

- I think that decision is personal for each parent and parent team, but likely more difficult for most women as physiologically I believe most women have a stronger parenting or nurturing "instinct" and drive than most men. Not all, but most. I think some women are better off working outside the home and saving their parenting energies for more quality time. Others would feel uncomfortable doing that. This may be related to their financial situation as much or more than their parenting "instinct". If my wife made more money with a career of more potential earnings I would have stayed home, but honestly would not likely have done as good a job as she has. She may have been less overworked with less stress if she had worked full time, who knows, but she would not have it any other way.

For our situation (for us the key is living UNDER our means) it was possible to have one primary full time outside worker and one primary full time person at home. I know my wife wonders what she could have achieved in the workplace, as she was always an overachiever (her university's woman of the year, athletic all-American, etc.), but she always finishes with "I made the right decision for me". My children have benefitted from that. I am always shocked, by women especially, that condemn other women for either choice. Really? Where is the tolerance?

- I grew up in a household where my mom did not have to work. I feel that households where one parent stays at home have a better opportunity to raise much more well- adjusted children. Notice that I did not say that the stay at home parent had to be the mom although I feel the mom being the stay at home parent is much more beneficial to the family unit. Mothers are USUALLY more nurturing and attentive than the father. Mothers seem to communicate vocally better than the father. Fathers tend to lead by example (children are to be seen and not heard/ do what your MOTHER told you to do). I know that these may be old fashion values but I think that the family structure has changed for the worse. We are and have been, for many years, raising out of control individuals. I think that the mother's role is to stay home and give the children the nurturing, education, morals and love that we all need but are lacking in these modern and sad times.

- I'm very supportive of mothers working outside of the home and don't believe it hinders the ability to manage a family at all. Like anything else, it requires planning and support to maintain a healthy balance of living. Working moms are excellent role models for young daughters and women who aspire to dream about their own future career choices. As a result, more fathers are assuming the role as primary caretaker in the home to insure the family unit has access to the best 'quality of life' possible.

- Work life balance plays a key role with how successful you are. Raising our children is our most important job (male or female) once again as I look at the people who I believe are great leaders they have a good work life balance that has been developed with support of others, usually a spouse or family.

- The question of children at home is irrelevant so long as the person be it male or female gets their work done completely and on time and contributes to the overall functioning of the organization in a way that demonstrates good corporate citizenship. I would put the same requirement on someone who has elderly and infirmed parents or a spouse.

- Having had female employees and managers, I have never had an issue with either. I work for an organization that has a lot of flexibility when it comes to where you work and hours. But, it seems as though females take more time off than men.

- Women who have children at home seem to work harder because they want the best for their children and take their jobs very seriously. They want to provide stability in their children's lives. However they tend to call out more if their child is sick, etc.

- In today's society, I believe most homes are a two income household. A woman should be given a couple of weeks off to have a child without losing her position with her company. If a woman needs to or chooses to stay out longer then I feel that a company should also be able to protect themselves with temporary or permanent replacement depending upon the needs of that company.

- Women who have children at home tend to be more conscious and conscientious about the need to balance priorities and multi-task.

- Men and women should contribute equally in the home..... meaning each parent should be willing to contribute financially (if needed), raising the family, and maintaining the home. I've never been a supporter of women or men being house wives/ husbands.

What are some of the biggest challenges you see today for women and men working side by side in the workplace?

- For women, lack of equal pay for accomplishing the same job tasks and the pressure (real or imagined) of needing to be as "tough" as their male counterparts in order to garner the same amount of respect in the workplace. For men, feeling threatened by the changing landscape as more women assume leadership positions and power. **I don't think there should be any problems with men and woman working side by side in the workplace.**

- I think that as long, as you have self-respect for each other you should have no issues. Having said that, I have seen men and women with less respect, mix business with pleasure. That can make the work place awkward for all the other co-workers around these individuals especially if you work in a family oriented environment, where co-workers meet spouses and significant others. If you are willing to compromise one value then often I have seen you willing to compromise multiple values.

- I think that the number one challenge with men and women working side by side in the work place is the lack of equal treatment. I work in a somewhat physical environment. Not what would be considered heavy lifting by the average male, but my female counterparts are always using their lack of physical strength to shy away from certain duties. If your job title is the same as mine and your pay is the same as mine then do the same job that I have to do, no exceptions. One other thing that is unfair is the difference in the biological make up of males and females. I have been in the situation, way too often, that when a female is having her menstrual cycle she becomes less productive and many times miss time from work and don't get me started on maternity leave. What are my equal situations compared to these facts of life??

- Intolerance of differences, just like between ethnicities, religions, etc. Some of this is generational bigotry, and reaction to bigotry, that is propagated by poor parenting and over-sensitivity (PC-ness), and well-meaning but philosophically wrong government mandates for "diversity". How about tolerance and cooperation instead? Let's team up and be productive. I do believe there is a human tendency to gravitate to people who are similar that we need to be aware of. Overall I think we should reframe the question: Stop thinking about the biggest challenges, and think about our biggest strengths. Focus on being the most productive. Race, gender, etc. does not matter. Be productive; combine our strengths into a team, that is the challenge.

- Without a doubt it would have to be communication skills. Nobody knows everything so when things come up that challenge us in the workforce it comes down to how well we communicate with our peers.

- As someone who has worked closely with women throughout my career in multiple organizations, the challenges are not gender specific. I am always interested in someone who has a high level of personal integrity, does their part when it comes to team efforts and helps to maintain a positive and supportive organizational culture. As I mentioned earlier, I have seen women and men successful in these attributes and both genders who are utter failures as colleagues.

- Actually, the way I see it, the dynamics between men and women in the workplace are all on a continuum. It's not so much women do this and men do that, but more about balance tendencies. In this women tend to fall closer to the middle (a combination of both versus either/or) more often than men do in terms of leadership traits, competencies, attitudes, and behaviors. Perhaps it's more a matter of comfort or discomfort about exhibiting these traits than it is about having them!

- There is still an imbalance with equal pay. If the female boss has done the job and knows the job then they seem to work out fine. When they have been promoted from the administrative side, there are growing pains and a lot more work is needed to gain the respect of peers and employees.

- Men don't see women as their equals but someone to hit on. When I see another man my thoughts are never sexual (yes, I'm heterosexual). But seeing another woman always sparks sexual thoughts.....I know, it shouldn't but damn it you want me to be honest.

    The other issue is equal pay for men and women. Some fifteen years ago, I took over a new group as part of an acquisition. The disparity in pay between men and women was huge. The first action I took with the group was to give the two women 20% salary increases. I never cut them any slack.....I expected the same of them as I did the men, so why not pay them the same.

How do you think women fare when competing for the same job as men?

- Unfortunately, the reality of sexism in the workplace still exists; however, the 'competitive playing field' continues to improve over time. Corporate philosophy is becoming more about who the best candidate for the position is and less about the sex of the individual. Compared to a generation ago, we've made great strides as a society but there is still work to be done.

- It depends on the nature of the position and the gender and race/ethnicity of the hiring manager. Since white males continue to be the primary decision makers in leadership positions in most public and private sector organizations, women (of all races/ethnicities) continue to have an advantage when the position is deemed to be a subordinate, administrative support position. However, the "ceiling" still prevails for women of all races/ethnicities when it comes to C-suite positions where there is a greater need for independent thinking and action and assertiveness.

- I don't think it is an even playing field when a woman applies for the same position as a male. I think the good old boy network is still strong and women and minorities have to fight twice as hard to get ahead. I think once you have broken through the barrier and have proven yourself, it might get easier; but, you still know inside you always have to prove yourself to be respected.

- This depends on the type of job. If it's a nice cushy office position women may be competitive with the males seeking that same position. If it is a job requiring being more physical, MOST women can't hold a candle to a male, there are a few exceptions.

- I believe that in general there are certain biases that people will always have; taller people usually are looked up to in leadership roles. Women have traditionally been in a supportive role but have made huge strides into the leadership across the USA in the past 20 years and that's been too long. Some women and some men can become great leaders I think the best leaders are respected because of their skills and knowledge and how they use them together for the benefit of the organization and not for their promotion.

- The playing field is still quite uneven. Being smart, doing your homework, and building credentials can help you to achieve success. Women tend not to be as competitive as men. As an example look at sports. Men get angry when they lose, but women kiss each other and console their competitors.

- In higher education and public health, women tend to significantly outnumber men. While there is some disparity as a function of discipline, women are generally successful when competing for vacant faculty positions. Our perspective is that since the majority of our students are women, we must have a high level of gender equity among the faculty ranks so we will go out of our way to identify strong women candidates.

- A lot of females who have been in organizations for some time are not a part of the "good old boys club". But the females I have interviewed lately have been better educated and more prepared.

- In the engineering industry, government agencies often give women an advantage, as many government employers are mandated or pressured to improve "diversity" instead of promoting performance based on merit. Some private employers do this too.

What would be your best advice for women aspiring to leadership roles in your organization?

- Be prepared academically and experientially (volunteerism is an excellent adjunct to work-related experience) in the role they're aspiring to achieve. Demonstrate a level of passion for the work and be prepared to share/demonstrate how their experiences would be an enhancement to the team and organization pursued.

- My advice is simply *do* the job as described. If brain power is required then apply yourself. If physical strength is required then apply yourself. I am a firm believer that a good leader leads by example.

- Be totally professional. Don't try to be flirty or over friendly, a man can over interpret your actions. Rumors can start very quickly. Just be professional and fair in everything you do. Your positive merits with be seen from the beginning and you should gain respect quickly.

- Understand that leadership (be it formal or informal) can, should, and does take place at multiple levels throughout the organization. Seek to obtain as much leadership experience and expertise as is allowed. Ceilings still exist- either decide to fight the injustice or find a viable alternative employer. There exists different states of readiness for social change and equity across and within organizations; a time for all seasons.

- Have a good balance of education and experience that blends well with your own personal work life balance, and always look for ways to improve your communication skills. With your feet set solidly on the ground reach as high as you want to go and go for it, but always be yourself.

- My advice would be no different regardless of gender. First and foremost, know thyself. Under promise and over deliver. Maintain a high level of personal and professional integrity. Support the people who work for you - don't throw a subordinate under the bus in order to make yourself look good. Walk your talk when it comes to organizational mission and values.

- Find a female mentor! Build a network of trusted advisors.

- Work hard every day. Learn as many other positions as possible, network and always be willing to volunteer for things outside your own position while mastering your current one. Make them know your value as an asset to the corporation, organization, or whomever you are employed by.

- Be the sharpest knife around the table.

Take on more than their fair share of workload.

Don't try to exploit being female........sleeping your way to the top doesn't work long term.

Act like a woman but think like a man.....no really, women should network more – hang out with the fellows and have a few beers, play some sports (golf or tennis).
Remain confident at all times. When vultures are circling, they can smell fear.....never...never show fear.

Remember, the first step to learning how to dance with one another in the workplace is to understand how the other person thinks, what they value and being open to their point of view. We don't have to always like or even adopt the "male perspective", just as they do not have to accept a "woman's perspective". But, if we take the time to understand and really *hear* each other, we go a long way to finding the common ground for success. If these men offer a small peek into the male mind, there is much fertile ground for the future. There's still bias to overcome as well. I thank each of them for their willingness to share.

The obvious and fair solution to the housework problem is to let men do the housework for, say, the next six thousand years, to even things up. The trouble is that men, over the years, have developed an inflated notion of the importance of everything they do, so that before long they would turn housework into just as much of a charade as business is now. They would hire secretaries and buy computers and fly off to housework conferences in Bermuda, but they'd never clean anything.
—Dave Barry

BLENDING MAKES MORE
THAN SMOOTHIES

Protein Power Smoothie

- *2 cups of milk*
- *2 tablespoons chocolate milk syrup*
- *1/2 teaspoon dry chocolate pudding mix*
- *1/4 cup peanut butter*
- *1 banana*
- *1 cups ice*

Place all ingredients in a mixer and blend until smooth. Enjoy!

You scan your kitchen cabinets and refrigerator for those special ingredients to give your breakfast smoothie an extra punch. Today you need high performance breakfast to give you an edge in meeting today's challenges. Each ingredient offers something different to stimulate your taste buds and energize your body. Six simple ingredients that cannot do the job alone, however blended together elevate you to a whole new level.

Why can't we think about the need for diversity in business the way we think about the ingredients of a smoothie? Unique characteristics and talents are much more powerful together than any one individual standing alone or with others who are all the same. Blending can maximize the potential of individuals and give an organization a competitive edge. It can also help an organization be more responsive to diverse communities and customers.

Yet we continue to choose our business partners who are "like us" because it's comfortable and differences are seen as a risk, including gender. Blending between the sexes is not valued as an asset unless it's in a Biblical sense. Women and men go to their respective corners and cannot appreciate that the same characteristics that make them different can be powerfully integrated for a shared vision and purpose.

Real strength is in unity! The secret to creating a high quality, high performance work team is the ability to use the strengths of each team member and the blending of their different viewpoints, personalities, cultures, processes, procedures, and operations into a tight, cohesive team that has bonded by overcoming shared adversity. To develop a strong team, the leader must be someone who is comfortable with that challenge – someone who can mold all of the different perspectives and personalities each member brings to the team into one way of doing business and establishing one organizational standard of performance. The leader must take the time and put forth the effort to truly understand all of the individuals that make up the team. Men need to understand the strengths of females on their team and the same of female leaders about men. Each attribute should be valued to move the organization forward.

Professor Judy Rosner, author of **America's Competitive Secret: Women Managers** gives an example of the attributes woman offer. Among the general male/female differences Rosner includes: Women are sensitive to subliminal cues; men pay little attention to subliminal cues. Research has shown that women can more quickly decipher facial expression, moods, and voice tones. This intuitive talent should not go to waste. This is a valuable tool that can be used as an advantage in business.

Here are some other attributes of women in business often mentioned throughout current literature:

- A collaborative leadership style
- People oriented-focused on relationship building
- Emotional sensitivity
- Leads by influence rather than power

- Comfort with ambiguity
- Comfort working toward win/win negotiations
- Process oriented
- Multitasking
- Strategic thinker utilizing logic and gut
- Creativity
- Women tend to use both hemispheres of their brains simulta-neously, so their approach is more holistic, while men use one hemisphere as they hone in and focus on problems.

On its web page (1/16/2007, In the News), The Paul Merage School of Business, University of California quotes one of their professors on their views about gender differences in business.

"Women look at the world with a searchlight. Men use a spotlight," says Rosener, professor emerita in the Paul Merage School of Business at the University of California–Irvine. "Men generally tend to lead in a linear, direct, top-down, command-and-control, results-oriented style, while women adopt a more interactive, multi-tasking, collabora-tive and team-oriented style, and are engaged in the process as well as the results". She stresses that her findings do not imply that one style is better or worse than the other.

Many organizations today are looking for transformational and visionary leaders with a style that is focused on outcomes and the development of subordinates (Bass, 1985; as cited in Maher, 1997). Bass identifies five main components to transformational leader-ship: charisma, inspiration, intellectual stimulation, individualized consideration, and extra effort. In the past, leadership qualities have traditionally been viewed as more masculine than feminine. However, the attributes of transformational leaders are more aligned with the attributes often considered female. The value placed on the caring and nurturing of the workforce has dramatically increased over aggression.

Additional research (Hackman, Furniss, Hills, & Paterson, 1992) implies that to be effective, leaders must display a balance of femi-nine and masculine behaviors. If these behaviors cannot be found in one individual, they must be present in a cohesive leadership team, giving credence to the value of blending in achieving organizational excellence.

We also need to embrace the different ways we communicate as an asset and not a liability. Traditionally, in the business world, the male model of authority was considered superior to the female model of collaboration. However, it's becoming abundantly clear that effective communicators are fluent with both styles. The key to success lies not only in recognizing and understanding the difference between the two styles of communication, but focusing on and creating for one's self a style that encompasses the best of both worlds.

Consider the following core characteristics of a well-blended respectful work environment:

- There is a high comfort level with diversity and differences
- Disagreements are not judgmental
- All values are understood and appreciated
- Stereotypes are checked and challenged
- Problems are resolved constructively
- Accomplishments are shared
- Supportive behavior prevails
- Disrespectful behavior is not tolerated

So ladies and gentlemen, make a new kind of smoothie- one that has the potential to propel your organization to the top using the best that all have to offer. Value each ingredient for its inherent worth understanding that blending can enhance the value three fold.

1 cup wisdom
2 cups compassion and the ability to listen
4 cups flexibility and willingness to value differences
1 cup internal fortitude for the journey
Enough ice to chill societal stereotypes
Blend well and enjoy a different world!

Out of chaos the future emerges in harmony and beauty.
—Emma Goldman

References:

Rosener, Judy B. (1995). America's Competitive Secret: Women Managers. New York: Oxford University Press.

Bass, B. (1985). Leadership and performance beyond expectations. New York: *Free Press.*

Hackman, M. Z., Furniss, A. H., Hills, M.) J., & Paterson, T. J. (1992). *Perceptions of gender-role characteristics and transformational and transactional leadership behaviors. Perceptual and Motor Skill*s, 75, 311-319.

Hosoda, M., & Stone, D, L. (2000). *Current gender stereotypes and their evaluative content. Perceptual and Motor Skills*, 90, 1283-1294.

Maher, K. J. (1997). *Gender-related stereotypes of transformational and transactional leadership. Sex Roles*, 37, 209-225.

Myers, D. G. (2002). *Social Psychology 7th Edition.* Boston: McGraw Hill.

Nieva, V., & Gutek, B. (1981). *Women and work.* New York: Praeger.

AN INCLUSIVE WORKPLACE

"We need to give each other the space to grow, to be ourselves, to exercise our diversity. We need to give each other space so that we may both give and receive such beautiful things as ideas, openness, dignity, joy, healing, and inclusion."
—Author Unknown

So, you have broken the glass (or in some cases concrete) barrier and have become one of a handful of women executives hired into your organization. You enter the conference room for your first Executive Team meeting and you are greeted by a sea of men all wearing the corporate uniform except their ties defining their individuality. The CFO has one with dollar signs and the COO has a hula dancer front and center - interesting choices. Quickly you realize that you are one of two females in the room and all eyes are upon you as you decide which seat you should take. Your mind tells you it probably would not be a good idea to sit with the other woman, even though it would have given you a sense of comfort. (I bet new male leaders never had these thoughts at all.) You decide to sit directly across from her, gaining comfort from her eyes that connected with yours the minute you entered the room. A quick smile lets you know she fully understands your discomfort and that she will support your first experience in the boys club.

The meeting begins with a discussion about the sport de jour with no indication of when it will end to get to the agenda. You wonder how quickly they would have gotten to the business at hand if the women had been having an open discussion about their last scheduled trip to the spa. Once underway, you quickly observe the highly assertive nature of the men trying to make a point, demonstrating their vast knowledge in front of the group. You are not even sure they know what they are talking about, but their posture denotes power and wisdom. At any moment you would not have been surprised to see one of them thumping their chest proclaiming their place in the organization's hierarchy. How on earth will you ever fit into this culture? Thumping is not your way. Working hard and demonstrating credibility through a much softer, yet effective approach is "your way" and more in line with the approach of a multitude of women in business. You wonder, "Without all the thumping and posturing will I ever be heard?" Most of the time, women executives have to work a little bit harder to be heard, often surrendering their approach to the ways of the boys club.

Therein lies the difference between diversity and cultural inclusion. This organization with all good intentions wanted to increase the diversity of their leadership team by hiring another female executive. Recruitment efforts were effective. Retention will be more difficult unless there is an increased sensitivity and value to the inclusion of women and "their differing approach and style" to the leadership table.

As a woman who made it to the C-suite, I feel compelled to contribute to creating cultures that value diversity *and* inclusion in the workplace. For all those women who come after my tour of duty as a health care executive, I pray they will not have to run the same gauntlet as I did to make it to the top. As you evaluate future employment options or are in a position to influence current organizational culture, it may be useful to know the clues to an inclusive workplace.

First and foremost, remember, diversity by the "numbers" (how many women in leadership positions) does not equate to an inclusive workplace.

Organizational Approach:

The ultimate objective of diversity is to create a high performance organization including competent, self-motivated employees and an inclusive leadership support system. Diversity must be viewed as *central* to that objective and not a separate initiative or program.

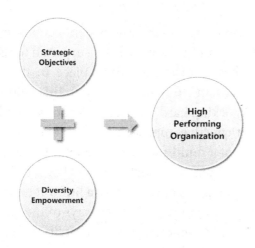

Leading Inclusion:

Leading inclusion requires a personal commitment (transformation), modeling inclusive behaviors, and influencing others (through accountability) to behave and produce results consistent with a culturally competent way of thinking.

Verizon offers a great example of steps they took to create a culture of inclusion and enhance the number of diverse candidates in their workforce. They have established an Inclusion Index which measures employees' sense of belonging and job satisfaction, while a Diversity Performance Incentive tracks workforce composition in each line of business. Senior leaders have 5 % of their pay tied to performance along both tracks (*Diversity Executive, Jan-Feb 2010, page 29*).

Clues to Inclusion:

- **Diversity initiatives are fueled by "good business" and designed to increase productivity and profitability in businesses and organizations**

- **Diversity initiatives are proactive and not reactive, using a variety of tools, programs, procedures and strategies to maximize each person's contribution**

- Leaders realize being different does not mean inferior. Different is normal

- Leaders realize that different people value different rewards

- Leaders value differences and strive to turn them into advantages by translating them into a company's assets

- Leaders recognize that new perspectives enhance problem solving and an inclusive environment builds respect, ownership and loyalty

- Leaders understand that highly trained workers will stay with organizations that are responsive to their needs

- Leaders think of gender inclusion as one aspect of a comprehensive management strategy to build effective cohesive teams

- Leaders identify issues that limit a women's ability to build lasting careers and addresses them systemically-including underlying systems, beliefs and behaviors that get in the way of women being successful. Discussion is deemed ok and critical to advancing a culture of inclusion

Beware of:

- *Golf Course Decision-Making-* corporate decisions made on the golf course or other select locations denote privilege for those participants no matter what gender, race or ethnicity. It promotes an outsider/insider culture which is counter to creating a high performing cohesive team. Corporate decisions should stay corporate unless all team members or stakeholders can contribute to the discussion.

- *Pre-determined Roles*- e.g. nurturer, firefighter or coffee-maker can quickly line up with historical roles held by women and men in corporate America. Team members should assume or be assigned roles that are based on their experience, expertise and a personal desire to fulfill the role devoid of gender bias. A man can be a nurturer and a woman can be a firefighter (crisis management) and either can make the coffee.

- *False Zero Tolerance*- lack of accountability or repercussion for discriminatory behavior. Unless overtly observed, many leaders make excuses for holding employees, including leaders, accountable for what is clearly outlined in the organization's zero tolerance policy. Inappropriate names or references about women coworkers are often passed off as a joke and never discussed as offensive and unacceptable. Remember, powerful messages can be conveyed with slight gestures or a few words. It's not always just the overt actions that should be addressed.

- *Identity Theft*- new leaders are often expected to assimilate to the behaviors of the dominant group, even in corporate dress and communication styles. Unique characteristics of the individual can be lost to group think. Identity theft often robs the group of the creativity and innovation that can propel the group to a whole new level. Women's voices are often silenced.

Assimilation Not Required-Professionalism Is!

One month on the job and my first Leadership meeting. As I entered the Board room I saw one of the largest board tables I have ever seen, enough to seat more than 25 leaders. Each leader moved to a seat and as I moved to one nearest the door, the Regional President asked for me to sit next to him, dead center. My immediate boss sat directly across from me. No one had told me the rules for this meeting, especially the unspoken rule that you never question anything the Regional President said. I was definitely in for a surprise when I crossed over into forbidden territory respectfully challenging some information presented by our Regional President.

For a major portion of my career, I had taught fundraising in the non-profit arena- a skill not often shared by other Health System CEO's. As our Regional President presented the action plan and challenges, I felt compelled to offer some differing insight that may be a more effective approach. The more I talked, the more the room got silent, with even some team members gasping as if I had committed a crime. I felt my boss kick me under the table to save me from myself and the anticipated wrath of the Regional President. It was too late. The words had left my lips. I had presented an alternative approach, offered factually for his consideration.

When I was done, no one except the Regional President would give me eye contact. It was as if they all knew I was going to be handed my job of one month in my hand and sent packing out the door. Even my boss had slouched down in his chair, head in hand. After a brief pause, the Regional President smiled and said; "I like your spunk and your recommendations are on target with where we want to go. Let's amend this plan to incorporate Jackie's action steps."

The next thing I heard was a collective sigh and one by one, eye contact resumed accompanied by nods of approval. My boss even sat straight up in his chair with the biggest grin, as if to say; "she works for me!" After the meeting I was surprised to get several thank-you notes from leaders in the group. They all had the same theme about being a courageous professional who had changed the cultural norm of the leadership team. Wow! Assimilation was not required…professionalism was the key.

In the face of "group think" we might be tempted to go with the flow and not make waves. The path of least resistance is saying "yes" when you want to say "no" and that road is always paved with regrets and mistakes. While compromise is good and a necessary part of healthy relationships in the workplace, no one should have to fully deny their feelings or thoughts and remain voiceless. You can stay true to your principles, responding factually and respectfully.

Embracing the Value of Mentoring:

During my career journey, there were very few African American female role models far up the food chain in health care. For many, this often serves as a deterrent to look at all the possibilities. It's sometimes hard to envision what you can be when you don't see anyone who looks like you in those roles. I feel fortunate to have had several role models to give me hope.

Having a same group role model is the ideal...but not the key. Having a mentor, someone who encourages, supports and pushes you professionally...even if they are different from you...is really critical. For the record, most of my mentors were white men.

Mentors, at least the significant one's in my life...saw my potential before I knew exactly what I could be. They opened doors and they were my mirrors. They helped me to discern what was important to me, so that I could pass on that passion to improve the lives of others. They helped me to navigate corporate waters and cultural norms I didn't understand. Mentors offered me a safe place to vent my frustrations and work though my challenges as a woman executive.

Mentors can play a significant role in the successful on-boarding of new female executives. New female leaders are usually in the minority and bumble around for months, sometimes years before they connect with other female leaders in the organization. A planned connection could increase the comfort level in the early phase of employment and ease the transition into and understanding of organizational culture.

Mentoring efforts can also take place outside of individual organizations, sometimes offering objectivity that cannot be achieved internally. These kinds of initiatives can connect female executives with other executives in similar roles, helping them to manage their careers, giving them advice and guidance and introducing them to other senior executives. Coaching, mentoring and networking programs have proven quite successful in helping female executives succeed.

We Don't Have to Fear Affinity Groups

The date had been set for the first *Ladies Night Out,* a gathering of the handful of female executives within the health system. Up to this point we had attended some meetings together, but rarely met to share our experiences or thoughts. Most of the time, we never even sat together…always trying to fit in with our male counterparts. During some larger meetings we had assigned seating, spread out around the room. I always thought they separated us to make it seem as if there was more woman than a handful out of a hundred plus men. Or maybe they thought we would multiple if we sat together or start a revolution.

The week before *Ladies Night Out*, rumors were flying about all the female leaders getting together and that the male leaders were not happy about this gathering. I was even approached by the CFO wondering what it was all about. I remember thinking how ridiculous their concern. The male leaders went out golfing, camping, fishing and to football games without the ladies all the time. They even talked shop and made decisions that us ladies heard about upon their return to work. However, when we wanted to have a bonding moment to enjoy each other's company-it was cause for concern. "What could they be talking about?" A revolution!

This kind of fear from the dominant leadership group is one of the main reasons organizations do not support the development of affinity groups in the workplace. In reality there is nothing to fear and affinity groups can actually advance efforts to create a more inclusive workplace. And when they work well, they can help companies recruit and retain top diverse talent.

An Affinity group is group of people who share a common interest, background or goal. This connection exists naturally in our lives…we like being with others who make us feel comfortable. That comfort comes from having something in common. As a woman from the Baby Boomer generation, I prefer hanging out with other women 50 plus, rather than the girlfriends of my daughters. We can chat for hours about our grandchildren and even comfortable shoes. Even strangers who share a common bond can gain a sense of comfort from eye contact alone across a crowded room. An Affinity group in the workplace just formalizes this connection with a purpose to enhance support, critically important for the less dominant group.

Affinity groups help increase employee retention by reducing the social isolation of being the only "one" within a department or division. A good employee affinity group can also boost diversity among a company's new hires. That's because under-represented employees are more likely to refer friends to their employer when they know that an infrastructure exists to support and utilize them effectively.

To avoid the pitfalls of poorly run affinity groups, have the groups tackle real organizational issues (e.g. recruitment/retention tactics for female leaders). This focus will direct the dialogue and minimize gossip and gripe sessions.

Affinity Groups should have a purpose that does one or more of the following:

- Supports diversity and inclusiveness
- Enhances the workplace
- Supports personal and professional development

A Word of Caution about Affinity Groups: Even though Affinity groups represent a wonderful venue to advance an inclusive workplace, companies should make it clear that those groups do not "deal with" the employer with respect to the terms and conditions of their employment, even as the company may encourage individual members to bring forward complaints through normal company channels.

Measurement and Accountability:

Explicit diversity and inclusion indicators allow organizations to monitor their progress and define priorities for action. Frequently used indicators include:

- The proportion of women in each level of employment

- Pay levels and attrition rates of men and women in comparable positions

- The ratio of women promoted to women eligible for promotion

- Retention rates of women and men in comparable positions

- Specific markers in employee engagement surveys targeted to reflect perception of inclusion by the workforce

- Focus groups offer additional insight into what is collected in the data (often best conducted by an external facilitator)

It is highly recommended that organizations use a variety of indicators-each could reveal a different underlying issue to address.

Men and women think differently, thanks to the vagaries of biology. But different outlooks and thought patterns don't necessarily ensure success or performance in the workplace. Emotional intelligence does.
—Jay Forte, President of Humanetrics

DEALING WITH REJECTION—
YOUR CUP IS NOT HALF EMPTY!

Dear to us are those who love us... but dearer are those who reject us as unworthy, for they add another life; they build a heaven before us whereof we had not dreamed, and thereby supply to us new powers out of the recesses of the spirit, and urge us to new and unattempted performances.
—Ralph Waldo Emerson, Author, Poet and Philosopher

Have you ever wanted something so bad and given it your all, only to be rejected or turned down? Many women, who have made it to the top of their profession, have hair raising stories about multiple rejections they have received along the way. The difference between those that make it and those that do not is the sheer internal fortitude to take each rejection as an opportunity to grow. That includes the ones that are so hurtful you want to erase them from your memory. These women didn't waste time looking at their glass as half empty, but half full with the potential to flow over the top!

Digging deep to find that space within yourself to grab that glass is not easy. Words of rejection by an employer (potential or current) can make you want to scream in rage or stay silent just to survive. Some fight hard to hold back the tears, vowing not to cry. Any of these reactions can further support the sexism or preconceived notions about women in the workplace. You may hear:

"I knew she would snap under pressure. This is no job for a woman."

"She's too quiet. I need someone more assertive for the job."

So how do you survive rejection for any cause and not let it paralyze your future? Some will go to that "happy place" in their mind to cope. I say, "Ladies, develop an I'll show you attitude!" Ask yourself, "What did I learn from this experience? What will help me the next time around?"

I remember my rejections in the workplace like they happened yesterday. The one that stays with me the most was handed to me by a hospital CEO I worked for in Maryland. It seemed that even my very best work never was good enough for him. It was as if my very existence was a major irritant. I worked very hard to become Senior Vice President and could not discern any other reason except my gender for his irritation. He certainly did not behave this way with my male counterparts, many with lesser experience than my own. I even felt like my mind intimidated him to some degree. And of course, I was no suck up. Integrity as a leader is very important to me. One day I was called into his office for an unexpected meeting. My gut told me it probably wasn't to congratulate me for a job well done. The fact that his secretary would not give me eye contact validated my gut. Within minutes of entering his office he informed me my job had been eliminated. And, as if that wasn't enough, he felt compelled to tell me that I should stop fantasizing about ever being a hospital CEO. I did not have what it takes. Just give it up!

As I walked to my car after gathering my things, a million emotions ran through my mind. And, yes, bumping him off was included in the top ten (smile). However, after I got over myself, I realized he gave me a wonderful gift. He taught me all those things I NEVER wanted to be as a leader. He also gave me the freedom to grow. He set me free. My growth would have been limited under his leadership. I have kept these thoughts front and center in my mind as a leader today. That rejection actually made me stronger. I would be dammed if I was going to let his words direct my future. I showed him by becoming one of the few minority women in the country to ever run a health system!

Rejection is no stranger to women in the workplace, especially those that aspire to leadership roles. Opportunities granted to our male counterparts continue to exceed those granted to women. Social norms, cultural stereotypes, power and privilege in organizations provide the "invisible foundation" for organizational decisions about which jobs and how much opportunity is suitable for certain types of workers. These decisions determine the ways that complex organizations structure work, creating barriers for women and keeping them from advancing in organizational "pipelines." For example, job recruitment and hiring practices used by employers often result in the initial placement of women in jobs that have short or nonexistent job ladders. In addition, enforcement of rigid work schedules, requirements of excessive time commitments, and lack of family-sensitive employee benefits constrain women's promotional opportunities as they try to combine jobs with the needs of their families. Ironically, low-wage jobs are the most inflexible and least likely to have benefits. All of these factors set women up for constant rejection and feeling devalued for their true worth. Sometimes it can make you feel like "what's the point of trying"?

My Daddy once told me, "Never let anyone tell you what you cannot be". Chase the impossible. Maintain your cool and integrity in the face of adversity. Cry with your friends who will love and support you. Then pick yourself up, put on your big girl panties and say…"I'll show you". Our life's journey is not always the straight path to your destination. The bumps and even times of rejection give us character and depth. Your glass is half full.

"When you're following your inner voice, doors tend to eventually open for you, even if they mostly slam at first."
—Kelly Cutrone, *If You Have to Cry, Go Outside: And Other Things Your Mother Never Told You*

SAFE LANDING—
RE-ENTERING THE WORKFORCE

Learn *from yesterday, live for today, hope for tomorrow. The important thing is not to stop questioning.* —Albert Einstein

All children are signed up for day care and ready for the new school year-check. MBA and internship are finally done-check. Three great prospects for leadership positions lined up-check. Biological clock ticking and husband ready for more-damn! Need a clone to pursue both dreams-absolutely!

Funny as this may sound, these are challenges women all over the country face every day. We work really hard to position ourselves for that dream job, then boom, pregnancy forces us to take a detour or put one of our dreams on hold. For all of us who have faced this reality for a multitude of reasons, re-entry into the workplace may be very scary, especially for leadership positions. Can we effectively hit the restart button? How can we assure prospective employers that our skills did not go south while we were focused on motherhood, school or other parts of our life that make us whole? Have we lost our competitive edge? How can we set ourselves up for success and a *safe landing* as a leader in the workplace?

The ease of re-entry is directly correlated with the length of time away from your field of interest/expertise. A visitor from a decade ago would hardly recognize the modern workplace with its PCs and business software, internet and e-commerce. Even factories and warehouses are driven by new technologies. Businesses use Facebook and Tweet key messages of the day to attract business or stay connected to their employees. The pace of change is high. Leaders of today are constantly challenged with staying current and relevant. This too is the challenge of a leader who is attempting re-entry.

Here are a few tips to help you with a safe landing to your next job in leadership:

- **Be an information sponge!** During your time away from your career, absorb as much current information as possible. Be disciplined. Schedule a date with yourself at least once a month to review an article, read a book, take a class or chat with a mentor about hot topics in your field. It's also a great time for self-reflection. Grab a pad and a pencil, and make a list of all the things you've done in the last six months to enhance your job knowledge and skills. Then, candidly evaluate your list. Would you feel comfortable showing it to your employer as an example of a good continuous learning plan? If yes, stay at it! If no…change it!

- **Update your resume.** Lead with your strengths. Don't forget about "transferrable skills". For many employers, soft skills, such as reliability, positive attitude, and an eagerness to learn is just as important as technical skills, often more so. Do not underestimate the skills we use in our everyday lives. Skills honed as a homemaker and community member can open doors and serve as the foundation of a rewarding career. For instance, homemaking skills require the ability to make decisions, handle responsibility and work with others. Share your resume with a mentor or peer in your field for an honest critique.

- **Find the right match.** As we take on new roles in our personal life, we may find that our interests or passions in our professional life may change. Re-evaluate where you stand in the present. What are your "absolutes" for a leadership role and what are your "negotiables"? Write them down. Now assess the leadership opportunities available to you. Do they match your current interests and personal boundaries? Remember, when you align your passion with the right organization, results for both are exceptional.

- **Prepare for the interview.** Try to anticipate questions a prospective employer may want to ask. Write down your answers. Practice with a colleague or friend. Some usual suspects include:
    o Why do you want to work for us?
    o Where do you see yourself in five years?
    o As a new leader for our organization, what's your vision for the next year? (This one requires pre-work on current corporate culture and strategic priorities. Make sure to check their web-site, public corporate documents like annual reports or financial statements and current employees you may know for intelligence. Google the company leaders.)
    o Tell us about a time that you made a bad decision or mistake and its outcome. (The wrong answer is "this has never happened to me".)
    o Know the job you are interviewing for! There will be questions that relate to that job. It is ok to request copies of the job description and even the tool that will be used to evaluate your performance before you are hired. Be prepared to address your strengths and areas of vulnerability.

Some additional questions you may not have considered:
    o Describe a time in which you had to adjust quickly to changes over which you had no control. What was the impact on you and your team? What was your response?
    o Describe a time when you communicated effectively, even when the person did not agree with you or your approach.
    o As leaders, managing conflict is an essential competency. Can you tell us about a time you had to resolve a conflict? Describe your approach and the result.
    o What techniques do you use to relive stress?
    o How do you decide what goals are established for your area (s) of responsibility? As a leader, how do you assure successful execution from the members of your team?

o Describe a time when you had to deal with competing priorities? What was your approach and outcome?

o Describe your approach in leading a diverse organization. This may be of particular interest if you are the sole woman of an all-male leadership team. Or, if you are not of the same ethnic or racial group as majority of the organization or leadership team. In this instance, use terms that align more with a culture of inclusion than diversity. It is more palatable for most.

- **Prepare questions for the interview panel.** Here are some areas of focus to consider:
    o Corporate culture/Strategic priorities
    o Healthcare and other benefits
    o Financial planning and retirement
    o Ob-Boarding/Expectations for the first 90 days
    o Continuing your education
    o Ongoing career path

- **Believe in yourself.** Hitting the pause button did not negate all that has prepared you for this next leadership role. But it will if you present yourself that way. Speak with confidence that you are ready, willing and able.

Believe in yourself! Have faith in your abilities! Without a humble but reasonable confidence in your own powers you cannot be successful or happy.
—Norman Vincent Peale, author

BUILDING YOUR LEADERSHIP MUSCLE

To lead people, walk beside them ... As for the best leaders, the people do not notice their existence. The next best, the people honor and praise. The next, the people fear; and the next, the people hate ... When the best leader's work is done the people say, 'We did it ourselves!
—Lao-Tsu

So what's the secret sauce to being a successful leader? What are the essential elements that will give you the edge you need. Here are some tips to keep you at the top of your game.

1. **Take control of your own destiny**. Never let anyone tell you where or who you should be. Chart that course for yourself.

2. **Maintain your integrity and honesty against the odds**. Hold on to what you value and it will sustain you over the long-haul.

3. **Believe that you can achieve the impossible**. If you don't believe in yourself, how can you expect others to believe in you? Highly effective leaders are those that are confident and courageous- they bring their heart and soul to work every day. It's not enough for you to just hold the title of leader, you must feel and act like a leader.

   At the most basic level, it's always fear that keeps us from achieving the impossible. Fear can stifle our creativity, prevent authentic communication, inhibit accountability, and stop us from taking risks. It's okay to be fearful sometimes. Acknowledge it and don't allow it to consume you.

4. **Know your own strengths and areas where you need support.** Great leaders are constantly growing and learning. When you claim to "know it all", you really have closed off yourself to possibilities that may be right in front of you. And, *do* take ownership of your own professional development. Instead of waiting for someone else to push you forward, look inward for those opportunities that will make you a better, more effective leader.

5. **Don't be a knowledge snob.** Be open to learning from a variety of sources. As a CEO, I learned from housekeepers and corporate Presidents. Both lessons were rich in helping me grow personally and professionally.

6. **Build support networks** and know that sometimes you need to go outside your current organization to find that support. It may also be a safer way to discuss those topics that may not be appropriate to have with a co-worker or even your boss. Over the years, I have developed a network of professional friends that I sometimes go to vent or check my own thinking. I trust these colleagues to give me honest feedback and to be my mirror when I need it. We all need safe mirrors both professionally and personally.

7. **Chase those jobs that bring you joy.** You will give and get more in return. Chasing just the dollar will leave you empty and sometimes with less in your bank account that you imagined. Doing a job that brings you joy adds depth and purpose to your work-life that will sustain you over the rough patches. It gives you wonderful memories that you can reflect upon when you reach a point (and you will) where you question "what on earth am I doing".

   To this day, in my office, I have mementos from previous jobs that remind me of those special moments or lives I have touched as a leader. I cherish each one. Just a glance when I am stressed helps me remember why I have chosen this path.

Joyful and purposeful work equals increased job satisfaction and is a contagious force for others who work with and for you.

8. **Be patient for the return on your investment in training and education**. My mother always told me, "Good things come to those who wait". We live in such a world that demands immediate gratification. We don't want to wait for that executive level job. We think an MBA gets us six figures as soon as we exit college. Please understand, great leaders were mentored and guided by other great leaders. They experienced failures and victories as they climbed the corporate ladder. That's how they learned what works and what does not work in certain settings. You cannot just graduate from college and be "all knowing".

9. **Be a good listener.** Sometimes as leaders you need to count to five in order to really "hear" what you may be missing from co-workers, your boss or employees. This is not always easy in the life of a female leader who is often described as the ultimate multi-tasker. We often engage in *passive listening*. That means only paying half attention to what anyone is saying. You are constantly having two trains of thought even during an active conversation. Body language even denotes passivity. Some very important conversations are conducted as we are desperately trying to exit our offices to get to the next meeting or crisis. Passive listening tells the one you are communicating with that you do not hold their thoughts in high regard- this may be an unintentional consequence.

    Active listening must be practiced as a skill. Active listening intentionally focuses on who you are listening to, whether in a group or one-on-one, in order to understand what he or she is saying. As the listener, you should then be able to repeat back in your own words what they have said to their satisfaction. This does not mean you agree with the person, but rather understand what they are saying. Active listening requires you to focus and stop all non-relevant work so that you pay attention to the person in front of you.

Pay special attention to where you are seated during the conversation. Sitting behind your desk denotes power. Power is also communicated if you stand over the person. Use eye to eye level as a guide. If you are not looking into the other person's eyes, figure out how to make that happen. As an example, sitting facing each other at a round table denotes a more caring approach. And, watch your own non-verbal cues. Do the words coming out of your mouth match your face? Lean forward to acknowledge active listening and nod approval, if applicable.

If the speaker is emotional, acknowledge the perceived emotion and reschedule if they need time to get it together. This also tells the speaker you care enough to address their emotional state.

Authors Susan and Peter Glaser, in their book "Be Quiet Be Heard" (2006) offer some great counsel on how to become a better listener. One situation that leaders often need great listening skills is in **responding to criticism.** The Glaser's offer these 5 steps to a more successful conversation. It is divided into two parts- getting more information and seeking out agreement wherever it exists.

"Step 1: Active listening- which includes a non-verbal curiosity and paraphrasing (reflecting back, restating the speaker's content, intent and feelings).

Step 2: Ask for details- requesting clarifying information

Step 3: Guess- When a speaker can't come up with specifics, you come up with one

Step 4: Agree with facts- be explicit in your agreement

Step 5: Agree with critic's perspective-acknowledge the speaker's perspective is reasonable (if it is so)."

If you are actively listening, there is little room for assumptions because you are constantly validating what has been said and assuring a common understanding on any agreements that are made. This includes those issues that do not have a positive outcome.

10. **Be willing to take occasional risks.** You don't have to jump off a cliff to prove yourself, but you can be willing to explore opportunities that are outside your comfort zone. Don't chase a job title that keeps you wearing the same comfortable shoes. Chase the job that allows you to do the things that you love, but stretches you, even if you have never been responsible for some of the job functions that you will be held accountable for. Remember, great leaders don't have to know everything. They just need to know how to lead.

    And once you are in a leadership role, **foster an environment of "emotional safety"**, where risk taking is rewarded, not punished, and where open, honest communication is the norm.

11. **Be a responsible leader.**
    a. You must own (support and committed to) your organization's mission, plans and initiatives.
    b. You must own all the duties and responsibilities that come with your job.
    c. You must own (be accountable for) the performance results of your team.
    d. You must own (admit to and fix) your personal mistakes and shortcomings.

12. **Take care of yourself and try to always look for work-life balance.** A better leader has found that secret sauce and holds it up as a work ethic for others. Identify those activities that replenish your energy and those that deplete you. Guess which ones should rise to the top of your to do list? Self-awareness is step one in prioritizing how you spend your time.

13. **Be the eternal optimist.** Negativity breeds more negativity. You could be the source of negative or positive energy in the organization's you lead. Your choice. Just remember, leaders set the tone for an organization or those who work for you. For those who are more pessimistic by nature, this is where men-

tors can help to support your optimistic quest. Talk to them about your views. Let them reflect back to you what they hear.

The challenge for many leaders today is maintaining a positive attitude during downturns. Yet, this is when a positive mindset is more important. Focus on solutions to improve the current challenge your organization may be facing rather than on the problems you may have no control over. Help members of your team do the same. Stay in touch with reality and always truthfully share the "state of affairs" of the organization. Followers will respect a leader that doesn't keep them in the dark.

14. **Hold the hand of others who aspire to lead**. Mentor often and for as many as you can. Remember, you have been given a great gift if you are a leader. Share that wealth. It will come back to you three-fold.

15. **Be choosey about who you hire and promote.** The more effort you put into hiring and promotion, the less effort you'll have to devote to managing the performance and behaviors of the people you bring on. Behavioral-based interview questions with a strong peer-based selection process will facilitate getting the best fit.

16. **Volunteer for the important opportunities at work**. Find your voice so you can effectively involve yourself in opportunities and collaborations. Push through the fear of failing that holds you back and raise your hand to take on that project.

17. **Be transformational.** Contribute your talents to a larger cause. Leave a footprint on the world or at least one other human being. When you contribute to something bigger than yourself, it gives your life a deeper meaning. And, you become a role model for others.

Steve Ventura, in his book titled "Lead Right" (2008) offers some exercises to *AVOID* if you want to build your leadership muscle:

- **Jumping** to conclusions
- **Dodging** your duty
- **Passing** the buck
- **Running** your mouth
- **Grabbing** the credit
- **Plugging** your ears
- **Throwing** your weight around
- **Side-stepping** problems
- **Stretching** the truth
- **Shooting** down the job
- **Bending** the rules
- **Pulling** others down
- **Breaking** your promises
- **Holding** others back
- **Playing** favorites
- **Just skating** by
- **Stepping** on others

In a keynote speech given by Joanna Barsh, on *"Centered Leadership: How Talented Women Thrive" (McKinsey Quarterly, September 2008)*, Ms. Barsh states:

"Women seek meaning in work while men seek status and pay and that gives women an advantage over men in the workplace. What drives and sustains successful women leaders is physical, intellectual, emotional, and spiritual strength that drives personal achievement and, in turn, inspires others to follow. The key is a sense of purpose, coupled with engaging activity, creating *flow*, a sense of being so engaged by activities that you don't notice the passage of time. Because of the synergy between purpose and an engaging activity, you will be happy and thus be performing at your highest level without burnout."

An article in the Harvard Business Review (September 2011), entitled: *Top Women Leaders' Higher Ambition Creates Equal -If Not More- Value than Men,* discusses the concept of "the higher ambition leader". According to the article, "a higher ambition leader builds a community of shared purpose, downplays his own role in the organization's success in favor of giving credit to his colleagues, and communicates actively with multiple levels of the organization to embed the focus and long-term goals of the company. Such leaders create shared values, strong emotional attachment, and high levels of mutual trust and respect to enable organizations to operate at elevated levels thus achieving the strategic vision and goals." They believe because women have to fight harder to achieve leadership status, they are "higher ambition leaders" and therefore more likely to succeed in business. Way to go ladies!

Notable Female Leaders (not all inclusive):

- Michelle Obama
- Shirley Chisholm
- Hillary Clinton
- Michaella Jean
- Margaret Thatcher
- Indira Gandhi
- Queen Elizabeth
- Golda Meir
- Rosa Parks
- Nancy Pelosi
- Harriet Tubman
- Madam C.J. Walker
- Victoria Woodhull

All the ladies mentioned above are leaders in their own right. They span the globe and have touched thousands along the way. They are truly transformational leaders. If their names do not ring a bell, I invite you to explore history. Each one will offer you wisdom on how to be an effective leader. Each one has discovered the secret sauce.

Do not follow where the path may lead.
Go instead where there is no path and leave a trail.
—Harold R. McAlindon

References:

Barsh, Joanna; Cranston, Susie; and Craske, Rebecca A.; McKinsey Quarterly (September 2008 issue); *Centered Leadership: How Talented Women Thrive.*

Galbraith, Sasha; Harvard Business Review (September 2011) *Top Women Leaders' Higher Ambition Creates Equal –If Not More Value- than Men.*

Glaser, Susan R. and Glaser, Peter A; *Be Quiet Be Heard* (2006); Communication Solutions Publishing; Eugene, OR.

Lyubomirsky, Sonja; *The How of Happiness: A Scientific Approach to Getting the Life You Want,* New York: Penguin, 2007.

Ventura, Steve; Lead Right (2008); The Walk the Talk Company, Flower Mound, Texas.

SPEAK YOUR MIND—
ASSERTIVENESS IS NOT A SIN

Everything you need is already within you. The beauty of life is that your DESTINY lies always in your hands. The time has come for you to STEP UP and BE GREAT! Write this down: My life is full of unlimited possibilities.
—Pablo Valle

Do you ever find yourself compromising your values to smooth out a conflict? Or do you worry that someone will judge you harshly if you speak up? Do you lie or gloss over the truth out of fear of rejection?

We all smooth over the truth and bend in our standards from time to time in order to reduce conflict and make relationships work. But when pleasing others becomes a habit you may find yourself resentful, which ultimately damages your relationships. Smoothing over disagreements and arguments can become more important than your own personal beliefs, eroding your self-respect.

Women, more often than men, find themselves in these awkward situations in the workplace and back off from standing up for themselves or what they believe in, even if it is for the good of the company. This phenomenon has plagued women in leadership roles for years because they truly believe they have a smaller range of acceptable behaviors at work than men. If they are too nice, they will be seen as weak or manipulative. If they are too aggressive, they will be judged as acting like men or typical bitches.

On the other hand, when men show traits of empathy, generosity and nurturing, they are credited for being progressive. If they are commanding, decisive and competitive, they are just a product of their testosterone and are seen as offering a competitive edge for the organization. Ladies, it's time to stand up and speak your mind…assertiveness is not a sin! And, if done well and using "respectful truth-telling", you can get the respect that you desire and, many times what you want. For leaders, assertiveness is an essential skill for success. Some even refer to it as an art to master.

Assertiveness means being positive and confident about ourselves-- our ideas, opinions and talents--and expressing these in the service of our values. It means acting on aspirations and exercising abilities, recognizing that each person is expressive and affirmative in a unique way. Assertiveness is not about being loud, rude, arrogant or disrespectful of others – rather, it is a direct, honest expression of your own feelings and needs. Unlike aggressiveness, it does not involve hurting another person, whether physically or emotionally, or violating their rights.

Assertiveness is the positive form of aggressiveness. When we are assertive, we have the strength to resist negative or hurtful influences. We think for ourselves, ask for what we need, and speak up to protect ourselves and others. When we practice assertiveness, we reinforce our self-esteem and self-worth. We aim to equalize the balance of power, as opposed to just "winning the fight", possibly through negative ways such as humiliating or hurting another person. Leaders who practice assertiveness correctly are more interested in negotiating a new solution with the other individual, than in just "I win / you lose".

Now and then, you're going to overreact or underreact. You'll blurt out something that you wish you hadn't, hurt someone whose opinion you value. The person with good assertiveness skills usually sends the right signals and gets the right responses. With assertiveness skills in their toolbox, women can learn how to better handle just about any situation that comes up—without seeming either shy or pushy. Although you might still be judged negatively by some for being direct and bold at any time, when you are diplomatically assertive, you are more likely to get what you want.

Very early in my leadership journey, I learned the difference between aggression and assertiveness. I was working as a nurse leader at that time and thought vocalizing my passion on a specific issue at a high pitch would show my strength of conviction and show my team I was qualified to be their boss. This was my first leadership position at the ripe age of 24. The position was head nurse for an inpatient unit at Johns Hopkins Hospital in Baltimore, Maryland. This was a job usually held by nurses with far more experience, averaging around 30 years of age.

Many on my team had already been questioning my promotion and what on earth I could possibly know at my age. I knew shyness would not buy me their respect or engagement in the work we needed to do on that unit to improve. Up to this point, all I had as role models in leadership were men. Aggression always got my attention from them, so I guess I thought it would work for me. Not!

At one of our regularly scheduled staff meetings, I unleashed this other "Jackie" I didn't even know was inside of me. Out of my mouth poured all the wrong words. My non-verbal expressions denoted more anger than passion and the tone of my voice was a major turn-off. I don't remember at what point I realized how immature I looked to my new team and to myself. This was not the real me, but a compromised version of me I thought I needed to be in order to be seen as a "leader".

The news of my failure, so early out of the leadership gate, rippled to other floors and among my peers. I thought my Nursing Director would change her mind and put someone more seasoned in the role. Instead she sent me a mentor. Her name was Mrs. Lingner. She was an off-shift supervisor who had about 30 years under her belt. She had broken in dozens of nurse leaders at Hopkins during her reign. She was direct and honest with a dose of genuine passion for quality care of patients under all that armor. Mrs. Lingner had extremely high standards for performance and scared me to death. Most nurses, young and old, prayed she would not be on duty during their shift. I am still not sure why, but she liked me. She told me she saw in me the hope of a good leader. I needed help, but I was not a lost cause.

In a closed door conversation, Mrs. Lingner schooled me on how to get the respect I desired from my team. (She first schooled me on what I had done wrong.) Of course, as with most leadership challenges, success is grounded in "how" you communicate with those you lead. She reflected back to me that my approach and aggressive style would only push my team further away from me and diminish any possibility of achieving employee engagement needed to achieve operational targets. I could have taken a more moderate approach and achieved a very different outcome. "Be assertive, Jackie...not aggressive. Don't talk at or down to your team. Be willing to listen to their side, even if you ultimately have to stand firm on your way of doing things."

Even though Mrs. Lingner passed away many years ago, I can still hear her words in my head to this day. She gave me different words to say to drive results and a better way to express my passion. I am so grateful for her mentorship and the impact she had on me as a brand new leader. Over the past 30 years, I have added to her list of "better words" and share it with you now in the hopes that you can add a few to your vocabulary as an assertive leader.

Assertiveness Tool Box for "Respectful Truth-telling"

Situation	Respectful Truth-telling
How to say "no"	No, but thanks for thinking of me. I am not comfortable with that. Your timing is not good, maybe another time. Thank you for this opportunity, but this really does not work for me right now. This is not the right direction for me. Thanks anyway.
Asking for what you want	I am confused, can you help me understand? Excuse me, can I have---? I could really use your support in--- Can we talk about an area I need some additional support or resources?

Response when you are put down in front of other people	(Privately) Can we discuss what happened in the meeting today? When you said-----it made me feel----. (Remember to only discuss how their remarks made you feel. No one can take that away from you). I would have appreciated if it could have been said to me in private if you are concerned with my performance. Thank-you for listening and allowing me to share.
Seeking Common Ground	I can see why you believe the way you do. I am concerned about that too. I want for the same things as you do. My solutions are different than yours because I came to believe something new from these particular experiences

Different types of assertive behavior will suit different people and different individuals. However, there are some aspects of assertiveness that are good for all instances – for example, don't be afraid to set limits and be firm in holding to them; don't back down at the first instance of pressure from others. Similarly, don't be afraid to say "No" – don't fall into the guilt trap – be honest with others if you are unable or unwilling to take on a responsibility, follow-through with a project, or agree with an opinion.

Being Assertive in Career Advancement

Speaking up for yourself to get ahead is not a honed skilled for most females in the workplace. My theory is that it is primarily because we approach new opportunities differently than men. We start from a base of "If I just do good work, it will speak for itself", or "I haven't been here long enough, I need to wait my turn". We need to think differently!

Ladies, we need to first value our own worth in the workplace and then know how to package that value proposition for our employers for advancement. Asking for a promotion or raise goes from self-assessment (the planning) and analysis (the basis for one's case) to:

- The right time and place for a face-to-face meeting with leadership.

- A summary of your value proposition- contributions (financial if possible). Speak clearly and factually—not with emotion or pleading.

- Asking for what you want. This is a specific request for what promotion and/or salary you want while being prepared to explain how and why you came to that conclusion, and why you are the best fit for that job.

- A willingness to listen to counter offers and to arrive at common ground (that means knowing what you would accept and what is non-negotiable).

Come prepared for the meeting. Write down the things you don't want to forget. Ladies, what do you have to lose? The ultimate answer is no. Rarely will it backfire if your approach is "respectful". You may even walk away, having gained a little more respect from your leader for taking a chance. You will feel empowered, even if you do not get exactly what you want. You got in the driver's seat, ignited your negotiating power and began to take charge of your own career destination. ***Assertiveness is not a sin.***

Never forget that you are one of a kind. Never forget that if there weren't any need for you in all your uniqueness to be on this earth, you wouldn't be here in the first place. And never forget, no matter how overwhelming life's challenges and problems seem to be, that one person can make a difference in the world. In fact, it is always because of one person that all the changes that matter in the world come about. So be that one person. —R. Buckminster Fuller

YOU ARE GETTING ON MY LAST NERVE—
DEALING WITH THE DIFFICULT EMPLOYEE

The better able team members are to engage, speak, listen, hear, interpret, and respond constructively, the more likely their teams are to leverage conflict rather than be leveled by it. —Runde and Flanagan

There goes Tina again with her eye rolling, lip smacking demeanor. She never has a good thing to say about anything or anybody. I know if I introduce something new or even a minor change, Tina will be the source of gossip about the injustice of it all. I get so tired of dealing with her craziness on a regular basis. She is "getting on my last nerve"!!!

I am sure you have dealt with many Tina's, either as a co-worker or as a direct report. In either instance, Tina would probably pass the sniff test as a difficult employee. Negative employee attitudes like Tina's are alive and kicking in the workplace today. They are often brought to work, get triggered by situations, and then infect others.

Learning how to deal with employees like Tina is an important skill for any leader. When leaders can successfully direct and support an employee's efforts to turn a negative attitude into a positive one, their stock goes way up with everyone around them.

So who are these employees that have given me more gray hairs than I can count? What's there problem? What are some of the key issues that most leaders at some point in their career have to face?

Behavioral Challenges:

Behavioral issues can include the person with excessive absenteeism or lateness, including those who didn't even bother to call to let someone know they will not be on time. It's the employee with continual financial or legal problems, the employee that has more than their fair share of accidents, the rule breaker, the one that drinks excessively or takes drugs. It's even the employee who lacks confidence and/or is a poor performer.

Attitude Challenges:

The issues that relate to attitude include the insubordinate employee at the top of the list, or it could be the one who just has a perpetual "bad" attitude. These employees can be change resisters and passive aggressive. It's the employee who undermines their leader with their co-workers or team, damages morale, continually complains or gossips creating constant friction. In some cases, it's the stressed out employee or one who suffers from some degree of mental illness.

Many behaviors of the difficult employee may even lead to formal discipline or termination.

A few examples of problems that could result in disciplinary action include:

- An employee who forgets to do an assignment or who flagrantly refuses to do an assigned task. (insubordination or refusal to accept a reasonable and proper assignment from an authorized supervisor)

- Receiving and making excessive or lengthy personal phone calls. (excessive use of the telephone for personal reasons)

- Speaking to a co-worker or supervisor or anyone using undesired and/or vulgar language. (use of profane/abusive language)

- Disappearing or leaving the work area without informing a supervisor for an indefinite or unreasonable period. (leaving work station without authorization)

The actual percentages vary from researcher to researcher about how many difficult or problem employees float around the workforce at any one time, but the range goes from 5 -15% with multiple variables affecting the number. For example, those who work in remote locations have lower numbers because there are limited options for employment, so people tend to keep their behaviors and attitudes in check. Turnover rates and corporate culture are also major variables impacting performance. If the culture has low tolerance for behaviors of difficult employees, the numbers are low.

The sad news is, regardless of percentage, it only takes *one* difficult employee to create havoc and discourse in an organization. And, despite your strongest wishes, these problem employees and the ripple affect they have on an organization will not go away. This is not a time for leader passivity. All eyes are upon you as the leader to see how you will handle the situation. Remember, the performance of the difficult employee is not a secret. Everyone is aware and hopes someone does something about them.

If you choose to ignore or have a slow response to a difficult employee, you could actually escalate an already tense workplace dynamic. Word of mouth spreads quickly, causing problems recruiting fresh talent into the organization or department- no one wants to work with this person. If the employee's behavior impacts work flow and productivity, now it has financial implications attached to it. Further complications can occur when decision making, scheduling or other processes have to be changed to work around the difficult employee. The more critical fallout is that there is a perceived lack of commitment to an organization's standards and work ethic because leadership is tolerating a behavior that is in complete violation of a condition of employment.

In identifying the difficult employee, a couple of distinctions must be made. There is difference is between a worker who habitually causes problems and the worker who happens to be experiencing pressures, stresses, or life challenges whose effects may be manifested in a temporary display of negative attitudes. Figuring this part out will determine how you will react as a leader. The second distinction is identifying the source or root cause of the problem. It doesn't excuse the behavior demonstrated or poor attitude, but it may affect your approach. For example, if there is truly an ongoing staffing shortage which continually puts undue stress on the staff, the solution may be a new staffing plan **and** counsel to the employee about appropriate ways to express themselves.

Once you have identified the source of the behavior and that there is a legitimate cause for action, it's time to get rid of that "pain" in your neck (not literally-yet). There are lots of steps before you would get to termination, unless the behavior is egregious in nature. Here are some action steps to consider:

Assessment:

- Be able to describe the problem with specifics about the behavior you want them to start/stop doing.

- Get all the facts –verify. This is especially important if you have not witnessed the behavior with your own two eyes. Even then, verify that your perceptions are real. Is this a temporary or on-going challenge?

- What's the downside of doing nothing? (Risk/Benefit of inaction)

- Listen to the employee(s) involved.

- Is skill or training an issue?

- Document your findings.

- Is this a valued employee you want to invest in?

- Check in with another leader, human resources or your boss for counsel before you approach the employee. Discuss your observations. Ask that person whether he agrees that the behaviors you outlined create a toxic environment for other employees and whether these acts undermine the organization's objectives.

- Decide on a course of action. What specifically, and most simply, would resolve the problem? What's the *easiest* solution? A conversation to share concerns? An apology? A meeting? Mediation? Try to keep it as simple as possible by choosing the easiest route first. No one approach may necessarily work for every situation encountered. But, again, whenever possible, start with the easiest approach first.

Communicate

- Set up a brief meeting with the employee to review the behaviors/attitude or performance issues of concern. In most situations, discussing a problem with the employee can usually result in a favorable resolution. Perhaps there was a misunderstanding, an oversight, or a lack of knowledge. Quint Studer, in his book *Hardwiring Excellence* (2003), describes a process for the meeting called **DESK**. The key elements are outlined below:

Describe- Describe what has been observed
Evaluate- Evaluate how their behavior made you feel
Show- Show what needs to be done
Know- Know the consequences of continued same performance"

- Set up a written and signed performance contract.

- Engage Human Resources if needed.

- Meet in a private location.

- Don't become overly emotional or lose your temper. A calm presentation is always more effective than an emotional or hostile confrontation. No matter how emotional or angry you may feel...stay calm.

Deploy Resources as needed

- Offer your support. Find out what motivates the employee's behavior. Determine whether he/she is just disrespectful or the behavior is the result of a control issue. Determine if they are trying to be cute or funny. Ask what you can do to help them change their behavior. Offer, but do not force, professional counseling if you feel the employee's personal issues warrant that. If his issues relate to the organization, coach him, listen to his feelings and mentor him toward a better outcome for him and the organization.

- Additional counseling or training may be needed (internal or external).

- Refer the employee to an Employee Assistance Program (EAP), which usually offers a range of counseling services including mental health and addiction services and support groups.

- An internal mentor may help, depending on the issue at hand.

- Address operational issues (i.e., staffing) if appropriate.

Follow-up on Compliance and Performance Improvement:

- The action plan will mean nothing if there is no follow-up at a maximum of 30 days out from the initial conversation and signed contract. Reinforce positive changes and identify slips back into the old behavior. Give prompt feedback.

Discipline/Termination

- Know and follow your own disciplinary policies. Review before your initial meeting organizational policies, employee contracts, and employee handbooks. Temporary circumstances may warrant a lighter approach, but consistent issues with the same employee require adherence to the "house rules". Otherwise, throw out the books and policies. They have no meaning or value.

- Engage legal counsel if needed.

- Terminate if no other action can resolve the behavior or attitude.

- Remember the confidential nature of the leader and employee relationship, especially if they are on the road to termination.

During the meeting remember to use simple, clear language, give concrete examples, and explain what makes their behavior, attitude or performance a problem. Give the employee a chance to respond, but not to argue. You want to be crystal clear about what improved performance will look like, and then give a reasonable timeframe for it to occur. It's very important to convey that you want the employee to succeed, but you do that best by being clear about what you need. Wrap up the meeting, assuring the employee that there will be both help and follow-up.

And please, document, document, document! Set up a file and keep records of all relevant documents and correspondence. Records should include factual written summaries noting date, time, location, and persons involved; memos and letters; relevant work documents; meeting notes; performance evaluations; and any other relevant paperwork to document your workplace problem. Keeping a paper trail is essential for providing needed evidence should legal action be needed down the road. Hopefully not, but you never know.

As for Tina…watch out, I have an aspirin and a whole new set of tools for you!

We know from our experience that it is easier to develop trust in another person or in a group if we believe that we can disagree, and we will not be abandoned or hurt for our differences. It is difficult to trust those who deny us the right to be ourselves. —Susan Wheelan

References

Patterson, Kerry, Grenny, Joseph, McMillan, Ron and Switzler, Al; *Crucial Conversations Tools for talking when stakes are high* (2002); McGraw-Hill; New York, New York.

Studer, Quint; *Hardwiring Excellence* (2003); Fire Starter Publishing, Gulf Breeze, Florida.

JUST GIVE ME MORE TIME!

Don't be fooled by the calendar. There are only as many days in the year as you make use of. One man gets only a week's value out of a year while another man gets a full year's value out of a week. —Charles Richards

Tick tock, tick tock…will this clock ever stop long enough for me to get everything done today? How many times have you had this thought?

One of the major sources of stress, anxiety and unhappiness for leaders comes from feeling like your life is out of control. You need to figure out ways to take control of your time so that you can take control of your life! This is a common challenge for leaders, especially women, who have all those additional roles to fit in as well. Of course, there are some things we can't change about they way we spend our time. We have to wait in lines, at red lights, for elevators and things like that. However, there is a lot we can do about situations at work. We must make better choices and learn to "just say no".

The first step is to figure out *where your time is currently going?* If you want to make improvements, you've got to know what to improve. To find the answer, I suggest you track your time for two weeks so you can make some educated decisions about what to improve. You will find that more of our time is taken by "how we do things" or losing focus on the most important priorities (main things) to drive our results. And remember, **80% of your results will come from 20% of your activities!** It's your responsibility to yourself and your team to know where your highest payoff activities are and eliminate as many as you can of the ones that yeild few results.

How We Do Things

Main Things Right	Main Things Wrong
Example: Run a productive and necessary meeting	Example: Waste two hours during an important meeting
Wrong Things Right	**Wrong Thing Wrong**
Example: Facilitate a great meeting that was not necessary	Example: Waste everyone's time at an unnecessary meeting

Now classify your activities- --Are you doing the main things (focusing on what's most important) and how well are you doing them? Most leaders have three areas where they can make changes that will lead to major time improvement: *prioritizing/organizaing, interruptions, and meetings.* This chapter will focus on best practices I found in each of these areas.

Tips:
1. **Keep paper moving!** Throw it away, act upon it, or put it in your reading pile. Shuffling and reshuffling paper from pile to pile with no evaluation or action is a waste of your time.

2. **Set aside some uninterrupted planning time each day.** This may be a difficult discipline for some, but 20 uninterrupted minutes planning yields the same results as 60 minutes of interrupted time. What a return on investment!

3. **Control your e-mail deliveries.** Do you check your e-mails every 5 minutes? Stop the madness!! Work e-mails into your schedule so that e-mails do not control your day.

4. **Keep track of who is interrupting you and why?** Then you can make some informed decisions about how to respond or address a problem. Even if you cannot eliminate the interruption-you can keep it short. A general rule: The length of the interruption is in direct proportion to the comfort level of the interrupter. Don't let the interrupter sit down and get comfortable in your office. If the interrupter does not get the hint that you are in the middle of something, stand up. It sends a signal that this will be very short and focused conversation.

5. **Schedule one-on-one sessions with your boss.** Using a predetermined agenda, keeps the discussion focused and within the hour scheduled. If pre-work was completed and sent ahead for review...even better!

6. **Ask your team: "What do I do that wastes your time and hinders your performance?"** Some of their suggestions may surprise you and could save you and your team valuable time.

7. **Make meetings productive, but short.** The average person wastes about 250 hours per year in unproductive meetings. Most meetings can be accomplished in half the time it is currently taking if everyone is prepared, on-time and focused. Using a standardized agenda with a focus on the strategic priorities will help to keep the focus on the "main or important things" and cut down on side discussions.

8. **Don't fall into the "perpetually scheduled meeting syndrome-** where you're having meetings just because they are regularly scheduled. Make sure every meeting is absolutely necessary. Routine meetings are only a good investment if they fulfill or move forward organizational objectives. Do your standing meetings have a charter that's reviewed periodically to see if it still relevant? Are the right people at the table for the objectives you need to adress at this point and time?

9. **Always begin a meeting by covering the most important items first**. This method assures you accomplish what you need to accomplish and you are not rushing through the "main" things.

10. **When people show up late, don't recap what you've covered.** When you recap, you are rewarding the tardy person and punishing the poeple who were on time.

11. **Start and end your meetings on time.** Think about it...you waste 30 minutes of productivity by beginning a meeting with 10 people three minutes late.

So, what will you do differently starting today! What are you waiting for? You just might regain back some precious time.

This time, like all times, is a very good one, if we but know what to do with it. —Ralph Waldo Emerson

STEPPING OUT INTO THE COMMUNITY

Service is the rent we pay for living.
—Marian Wright Edelman,
President of the Children's Defense Fund

What are you doing for others?
—Dr. Martin Luther King, Jr.

The phone rings in the midst of another crazy day as a leader in your organization. You shuffle the papers on your desk and answer to hear the voice of a Board member soliciting your participation on a community board. You already serve on two other boards and don't know how you can possible fit in another. You are not sure how to tell your Board member "no" without hurting his or her feelings. How did you find yourself in this situation? 16 hour days cannot possibly get any longer. This is often the plight of a leader, especially a successful one. And, female leaders are in demand on community boards which have historically been comprised of all men.

For most of us who signed on to the job of leadership, we probably did not see in the job description the expectation of community service. However, it is and has always been the mark of true leadership-the ability to give back **unconditionally**. It's that steadfast dedication to improving the community in which you work and live for the future and, using your leadership skills to be a positive role model to others. Community service can take many forms: individual mentoring, empowering groups, fund raising, teaching, participating in community projects (i.e., *Habitat for Humanity*) and a variety of other support services. It is a reciprocal proposition, with both parties gaining from the experience.

About one in three American adults currently participate in community service, and studies show that people who donate their time not only help the community but also gain work experience, meet new friends and improve their own health. Community service has been shown to improve self-esteem, reduce heart rates and blood pressure, increase endorphin production, enhance immune systems, reduce stress, and combat social isolation (Corporation of National and Community Service, 2012).

The Business Times (March 6, 2012) states, "One estimated dollar value of volunteer time is $21.36 per hour. That estimate helps acknowledge the millions of individuals who dedicate their time, talents and energy to making a difference. Charitable organizations use this estimate to quantify the enormous value volunteers provide. According to one estimate from the Corporation for National and Community Service, about 63.4 million Americans — nearly 27 percent of the adult population — contribute a collective 8.1 billion hours of volunteer service worth $169 billion a year". Wow, that's quite an impact!

However, the value of community service goes so much further than can be estimated in dollars and cents...it has a dramatic impact on every life touched along the way. In some cases, leaders have a unique opportunity to change the course of events for an individual from one of despair to one of hope. Sometimes, it can be as simple as telling our story to give someone else the strength to travel a difficult path to success.

The power of sharing your story really hit home to me after delivering a lecture to a group of students at an area college in Pennsylvania. It was a voluntary commitment as a part of my personal quest to try and offer some contribution to our leaders of tomorrow. The topic was on diversity and inclusion and the impact they can have in making a difference in their workplace and personal lives. I challenged their current world view on the topic and shared my journey as a woman and a minority in leadership.

The dialogue was spirited; as they had lots of questions about the challenges I faced to become a CEO in the health care industry. They also expressed concern over the oppressive nature still inherent in their parents and others throughout the community in which they lived and worked. As on many occasions when I speak publicly, I walked away wondering what impact I really had. I wondered if my words reached at least one individual and made a difference in their lives. About a year after I gave this speech to the students at that small college in Pennsylvania, I got a care package from their professor.

The care package of about 20 essays came with a note which said, "Jackie, I have been meaning to send these to you after your lecture at the college. Get out your tissues, because these essays from the students will touch your heart. This was an assignment after your lecture about their lessons learned. Enjoy." Here are just a few samples of what I received.

Student #1

I heard a song on the radio as I was driving home from class last Saturday reflecting on the class and the discussions that we had as a group. I felt that this song reflected some of what Jackie had expressed that day. The song says, "There's always gonna be another mountain. I'm always gonna wanna make it move. It's always gonna be an uphill battle, sometimes we might have to loose. It ain't about how we're gonna get there. It ain't about what's waitin' on the other side. It's the climb". (Sorry about the grammer, I didn't write the song). I thought this is a lot of what Jackie was saying. There will always be challenges in life both personally and professionally. It's not about what the challenge is, it's about how we meet the challenge. How will we act, what will we do to make a difference during the journey. People may try to break us along our journey, and others will look towards us as leaders on the journey. We must lead by example. We must be the light that draws others to us to climb the mountain. Sometimes we might feel like we are climbing the mountain alone, but there are always others who join us along the way in life.

As leaders, we must show others respect, and others will learn to respect each other by our example. If we respect diversity, in terms of a celebration of the differences in each other and the different positive attributes that we have, then others around us will see the light. We must make others feel more comfortable, and not be afraid to ask questions. We must be aware of our own insecurities, and face them. We must realize what we do not know, and ask these questions. We can only learn from this, and others are usually happy to share and to help.

We should not stand by and watch others be persecuted or disrespected. Instead we should confront the persecutor, because "if we permit we promote", as Jackie stated. There should be zero tolerance for this type of behavior. It may be difficult to stand up to the offender, but is necessary to prevent further damage and disrespect. This type of behavior can be toxic to an organization, and should not be tolerated.

As a result of this class, I plan to ask more questions. I work with many people of different ethnic and racial backgrounds, and there are many things I do not know. I have asked many questions over the years, but have many more to ask. I plan to be more open minded and try to see things more from the other person's point of view.

Student #2

With the week's reflection focusing on the presentation of Jackie Gaines, I found myself to be more troubled than I thought I would have been. I look at others for who they are, based on my exposure to them and personal interaction. I pay particular attention to the set of skills they bring to the table, past performance and/or ability to do the job. Never does sex, or skin color enter into the decision making process. I never thought of myself as having blinders, however now, to some degree, even if due to pure ignorance I just might (have blinders on). It is the individual person that I take into account when I consider the above; however, when considering the big picture; the entire group or population I find I have some bias. She opened my eyes to see that diversity is so much more than culture or color. I now view being truly diverse, as having your eyes open not only to cultural and color differences but to the variety of differences between people and especially in the workplace diversity encompasses race, gender, ethnic group, age, personality, tenure, education, background and more. Diversity not only involves how people perceive themselves, but how they perceive others. These perceptions affect our interactions.

What can I do now as a leader within my organization; I can make sure I focus on maximizing the ability of all my employees to contribute to organizational goals. Being able to provide what is needed to succeed. Today, we have such a diverse workforce we ought to be more consider-ate of the needs of the varying population. I can work to influence my leadership to become more accommodating and introduce flexible work-ing hours. Maybe we need to consider hiring part time mothers with school age children between the times of 10 and 2. For a call center this covers our busy times through the lunch period and allows for mom to put their children on the bus and be there get them off the bus.

I can better recognize the challenges such as communication - cul-tural and language barriers, because ineffective communication of objectives results in confusion, lack of teamwork, and low morale. By simply acknowledging that this possibility exists can be a foot in the right direction. The resistance to change, another challenge that will be more difficult to overcome, there will always be employees who refuse to accept the social or cultural makeup and this mentality only stifles new ideas. Understanding that employees from diverse backgrounds can bring new talents and experiences which offers a greater variety of solutions to problems. It is my role to include these various talents in meetings and decision making activities when I can. I will do my best to continue to develop honest and open relationships with staff. I believe in the zero tolerance approach and realize to really be effective this needs to be a corporate initiative. I may not tolerate comments or actions within my own department but do have little control over others. Therefore, my role will be to continue to educate and influence other leaders as best I could. Continue to ask questions and be open to answers because it is true, we'll never stop making mistakes, but it's how we deal with them.

Recognize the blinders are on is the first step to taking them off.

Student # 3

When I ask myself if I am open or closed, I guess I find that I am not 100 percent of either. My agency has employees from diverse backgrounds. I am open in that I do not let a person's race or ethnicity affect how I treat them. I have become very close friends with two of my coworkers outside of work, one is African American and one is Latino. I just think of them as friends. Nothing else really matters. I have, however, stood by while they were harassed by a previous supervisor. He would use racial slurs that I have not heard in twenty years. Things I did not know people even said anymore. I was afraid that if I stood up to him, I might jeopardize my job. Eventually, he was fired for his inappropriate treatment of employees. Now that I listened to Jackie, I would definitely speak up in the future. In other ways, I still think that I am closed. If I see a black person in my neighborhood, I have to admit that I am uncomfortable with that.

I think that things have progressed with each passing generation. My kids attend the same high school that I attended. It is more diverse than it was when I was a student there. I noticed that my kids do not seem to notice the differences in other students' race and ethnicity because they are exposed to a diverse population of students. People were definitely more interested in your ethnic background when I was growing up, but that does not seem to be much of an issue anymore.

I recently left my church that I had been attending for the past twenty four years. It is a strict Baptist church that stresses one way of thinking and believing. As my children got older and were able to understand more about what was being taught, I began to realize that it was not teaching them to respect other people's beliefs. The goal there was to impose your beliefs on others and get them to convert. They even frowned on letting your children befriend others with different beliefs unless you were trying to convert that person. It was very hard for me to leave. I took a lot of heat from family and church members, but I think I made the right decision for my children. I think I am becoming more open.

Student #4

Saturday's class with Jackie was not what I was expecting. I expected her to talk about just her experiences and leave the discussion at that. I was pleasantly surprised how her talk evolved into a discussion. There were many things that I picked up that will not only be relevant in my professional life, but also on the personal end of things.

Ask why. It sounds simple and in theory it is simple to do. Sitting in a staff meeting questioning why we do things that have been done the same way for years is another story. I often times find myself sitting and wondering why we do things the way we do here at King's.

I have found that it is easier to sit back and just let things continue to happen as they have in the past, but that is not something that I want to let happen in the future. I need to question why we do some of the things that we do. I need to do that in my personal life as well to really get to the bottom if why I do some of the things that I do. If I am doing something because that is what I have always done and never really questioned why, then there is a good chance that I am missing something and there could be an easier or better way to do things.

"If we permit it, we promote it." This could not be more true in today's society. We are seeing what happens when things go uncorrected for so long with our economy. Many of these situations could have been prevented or stopped earlier on if those in positions of power had only spoke up and said something. Those who have the power often times are not the ones to call attention to our problems. I understand that it is easier to "choose your battles" in many situations and avoid a confrontation, but we can't accept that anymore whether it be in healthcare, education or government. We need to make sure that we are aware of what is going on and we are okay with what is going on. Turning a blind eye and ignoring things is not going to work anymore. We need to make the tough decisions to get our economy and healthcare back on track. Healthcare should be a patient centered system, but it isn't. This is not going to be easy to correct the mistakes that have been made, but it is something that we need to do.

Hearing Jackie talk about the 'outsiders club' makes a lot of sense to me. I am a white male, decent job, highly educated and very easy going. I thought that moving out here from Pittsburgh it would be very easy to meet new people and 'fit in.' It surprised me when I got here to find people were not as accepting of me because I was not from this area. I can only imagine what Jackie went through and I agree that it is easier to move to a place where you can be happy instead of changing how things are in Northeastern PA. I have heard that most people come here, get an education and then leave and go to put their education to use elsewhere. I don't see this area as being very welcoming and that is negatively affecting everyone in one way or another. If the culture does not change I doubt the depressed downtown part of Wilkes-Barre will ever fully recover. I do not know if I can fully change the culture or mindset of those from this area, but what I can do is be welcoming to people and treat them how I would want to be treated.

The struggles that Jackie has encountered will now serve as a learning point for those who she speaks with and those who read her book. Jackie has paved the way and opened doors that 30 years ago would not have been thought of. She is a very dynamic speaker and has opened my eyes to many different things that I can do to in my everyday life to make much needed changes.

The professor was right! I needed the whole box of tissues. It just goes to show you that you never know who's listening and the impact you can have that may leave a footprint on the future. No matter what draws you to community service, it leaves you smiling from the inside out. This is especially true, if you choose wisely, how and what organization to offer your volunteer service. My advice is to follow your passion. The number of organizations you choose annually should be balanced with your workload and personal life. If all you have time for is one community board, just do one. You will have more impact than spreading yourself too thin.

And, enjoy being an active participant in offering "random acts of kindness". That's a great side benefit of being a leader. And remember, you can start earning this benefit even without leader shoes.

The true meaning of leadership is service.
—Carter Woodson, educator

Plant a thought, harvest an act, harvest a habit, harvest a character. Plant a character, harvest a destiny. —Sacagawea

---

References:

The Business Times (March 6, 2012), *Value of Volunteering: Acts Small and Large Priceless*

The Corporation of National and Community Service (2012-on-line resource)

THE FLASHING LEADER—CHALLENGES FOR THE MENOPAUSAL LEADER

Over the next few years the boardrooms of America are going to light up with hot flashes. —Neil Sheehan

It's 1 pm in the afternoon and you are standing at the podium getting ready to address your leadership team of seventy leaders. You are wearing your favorite linen suit, looking at the top of your professional game. Then you feel it. It starts at the tip of your ears and begins to move down the rest of your body. You think to yourself, "Not now! Just let me get through this meeting."

There is your albatross, that pain in the butt hot flash! If you sweat, it will definitely show in the linen suit. So you jokingly make fun of yourself having a "moment" and you begin to do the 55 year old strip-tease. The coat comes off (at least until it passes) and there you stand in your silk tank top and skirt. You have learned to dress in layers because you never know when or where this striptease will need to be repeated. And, your leadership team just looks at you and smile. The more mature women in the room understand. The younger ones like your tank top. And the men are clueless and find your behavior weird. If it's a really bad "moment", the sweat may even begin appear on your forehead. Now, you are really distracted and hope no one else notices as you reach for that tissue to dab as you begin your opening remarks.

Here's another scenario: You are having your monthly supervision meeting with one of your direct reports, when in mid-sentence your mind goes blank and you have to start the conversation over. You pray the person you are talking to doesn't notice or think you are crazy.

Welcome to the world of the menopausal leader.

So how do professional women cope with the gifts of menopause that can include memory loss, mood swings and depression, along with the dreaded hot flashes? By suffering (and perspiring) in an embarrassed silence. This rite of passage for women is not the same for us all. Some women seem to sail through the hormonal turmoil that marks the end of their fertile years (average age 51), but for others, symptoms such as hot flushes, mood swings and memory loss can be so dire as to make life intolerable.

For women in demanding jobs like senior management, this time of life can be particularly tough. At work, women often do their best to hide their symptoms, despite feeling lousy much of the time. "The change" is still something working women prefer to keep to themselves, out of embarrassment and fear of being seen as less competent. It doesn't help if colleagues add to these feelings with off colored comments about women going through this phase in their lives. Menopausal symptoms are often seen as a stigma, at odds with the self-confident, professional image women want to convey at work.

However, menopause is a natural, normal phase in a woman's life. It is clinically defined as the stage in a woman's aging process when her ovaries stop releasing eggs. Menopause can occur naturally or may be induced by surgery, chemotherapy or radiation and is considered complete when a woman has been without her period for one full year. The age for menopause ranges between 40 and 58 with an average age of 51 -- many years short of the national retirement age of 65.

Currently, women comprise almost half of U.S. workers, and recent trends show that female Baby Boomers (those born between 1945 and 1960) are expected to remain in the workforce past retirement age. The number of menopausal women is also growing rapidly. According to the American College of Obstetricians and Gynecologists (ACOG), the first wave of Baby Boomers are now entering menopause and it is estimated that another 20 million will reach menopause in the next decade. All told, these facts and figures combine to make menopause, its symptoms and treatment, a significant health issue.

What Can You Do?

Our mothers who worked had to grin and bear the challenges of menopause, but today's women are seeking ways to cope. Here are some suggestions. You do not and should not give up your day job.

- Acknowledge that menopause is a natural part of life and not something that must be hidden at work. Don't fight the inevitable.

- Have honest conversations with your employer about work accommodations as appropriate.

- Keep a diary of menopausal symptoms over time, and discuss them with a health professional

- Discuss the benefits and risks of hormone therapy with a health professional

- Understand individual risk factors and health history

- Explore differences among treatment options

- Consider meeting with a physician who specializes in menopause

- **Symptom Challenges:**
  o If you feel a **hot flash** coming on, deep breathing may help minimize its effect. If you can't excuse yourself from the boardroom, try quietly breathing in for six counts, holding for six counts, and then exhaling for six more. And if you don't feel cooler, at least you'll be a little calmer. Remember, a hot flash only lasts a few minutes…this too shall pass.
  o Lightweight, loose items make better wardrobe choices for menopause management. If it's chilly outside, layer your clothing so you can peel off an item or two as needed. The tank and jacket really do work!

o It's common to feel nervous, irritable, and tired as you're going through menopause — which can make you a less-than-pleasant business professional, especially on days when you have to deal with difficult clients or complete "just one more" task for your boss. Create a focus for yourself when you feel that **mood shift** coming on...a quick walk outside or shutting your door to close your eyes for five minutes of quiet can often get you quickly in a better space.

o For **memory challenges**, leave notes for yourself or keep a leadership journal. Once journals become a natural part of your leadership style, no one will know that it's because you can't remember all the details in your head. You would be surprised how many younger leaders have copied or asked me to teach them journaling because they thought it was a brilliant leadership tool for success (Fooled them, huh?)

o Take a day off to address symptoms that are particularly intense. A break in the stressors of work may be all you need to get back on track.

Recommendations for Employer Support

With any longstanding health-related condition, sympathetic and appropriate support from employers is crucial in order to provide women with the help they need. It is widely thought that such support encourages employee loyalty and facilitates continued engagement at work. But employers can only be sympathetic to these needs and make suitable work adjustments if aware of a problem. People are more inclined to disclose if they regard leadership as supportive and there is a culture of openness about health issues.

However, in many workplaces there is very little awareness of menopause as a potential health issue; it is a 'taboo' topic. Women are often embarrassed to disclose their problems or fear that their bosses would be embarrassed if they raised the subject, particularly if those they report to are younger than them or male.

Support for menopausal women can be increased, through more non-judgmental education and awareness, more flexible working hours and, crucial, improvements in work place temperature control and ventilation. Personal fans aren't bad either! In addition, some organizations have focused training for leadership on how to work with an aging workforce. Others have facilitated the setting up of informal support networks to help women going through the menopause. Offering women more control over the temperature of their immediate working environment can be helpful. But above all, it is important to listen to women and respond sympathetically to requests for adjustments at work. Boomers **will be** in greater numbers in the workplace. As a matter of fact, they will be the norm. Therefore, menopause will be the norm. Imagine that!

Male menopause is *a lot more fun than female menopause. With female menopause you gain weight and get hot flashes. Male menopause - you get to date young girls and drive motorcycles.* —Rita Rudner

References:

Lewis, Reynolds, (August 2008), The Seattle Times, *Working through on the Job Menopause.*

BEING MY OWN BOSS—
THE ENTREPRENEURIAL

Experience. Dream. Risk. Close your eyes and jump. Enjoy the free-fall. Choose exhilaration over comfort. Choose magic over predictability. Choose potential over safety. Be Bold. Be Fierce. Be Grateful. Be Wild, Crazy and Gloriously Free. Be You. —Anonymous

How many times have you ever thought of running your own business…being the Queen of your own universe? For me, I know I have tried my hand at a couple of things I thought (ok, wished) would allow me to be my own boss. I remember when I was home after the birth of my first child. Flower-making was my thing. I would sit in my living room floor for hours with baskets, wire, dried flowers and make arrangements to sell to family and friends. Somewhere in my young mind, I actually thought it would magically take off into a sustainable business well into the future. No business plan, no consult, I hadn't even read a book…but I was on my way. I got a few sympathy sales at my husband's job, but then it died. There went my flower shop…my shot at independence. Sad story, but shared by many women throughout the country.

If I were a younger mom today, I probably would fall into that new definition of *mompreneurs*, a business owner who balances the roles of mom and entrepreneur. Palmer (2011) states "the mompreneur movement is one steadily growing in the U.S. as mothers try to find ways to make money, express their creativity or business acumen, and also to parent their children. They are a relatively new trend in entrepreneurship, and have come to increase prominence in the internet age, with the internet allowing entrepreneurs to sell products out of the home rather than relying on foot traffic to brick-and-mortar business".

Whether you are a mompreneur or a woman on a mission to make her business idea a reality…dream, do your homework, plan carefully, get advice from someone you trust, make sure your finances are in order and go for it! Some of the most successful businesses today, started with someone's dream. Why can't women start to play the entrepreneurial game?

Know the Rules of the Game! Here are some tips to get you started.

Step One: Start with Passion

Not sure where to begin? Look inside yourself and identify those things you love. What do you like to do? In other words…start with things you are passionate about. When your work and passion combines, you have discovered a powerful sustainer for the future. It will fuel your creativity and offer credible testimony to the target audience that you really believe in what you are selling. Yes, marketing your business is an art…but marketing takes on a whole new meaning when your passion can be palpated.

Step Two: Identify Your Target Audience

Who would benefit most from your product or service? Have you considered the depth of the market? How about how long its appeal would last? For example, the interest span of today's teenagers is short lived. What may be popular this year will move quickly to another new fad. Geography may even be an issue. What may sell in one location, may be of no interest in another. You can't sell grass seed to folks who live in condominiums.

Step Three: Identify Your Hook

What exactly are you selling? Are you the *first* or are you trying to enter a crowded market? Of course, if you are the first, your product must be something that your target audience would value or find unique enough to purchase. You also may be able to find a niche in a crowded field of products or services. A good example of this is found in the hotel industry. Some bright person thought of destination, all-inclusive hotels. Now, they are the hottest thing for vacations all over the world. You should be able to articulate in just a few sentences why the person(s) you are addressing really needs what *you* have to offer.

Step Four: Do Your Homework!

Now that you have a great idea, it's time to test that theory against the existing market. Identify your competition. What's their edge over your idea? How will you separate your product or service from theirs? In this age of internet, some of the homework can be done right on line, without hiring a firm to do it for you. You are trying to glean specific information about your target market and the key factors that influence their buying decisions. Market research can be casual and limited in scope and, although it may not be "statistically significant" research, it can still be valuable.

There's a lot the internet has to offer. This is information others have acquired and already published which you may find relevant. Access to this market research data may be yours for the asking and cost you only an email, letter, phone call, or perhaps a nominal fee for copying and postage. Much of it is entirely free. Some sources to consider include- trade associations, government sites (Small Business Administration, U.S. Census Bureau), Chamber of Commerce.

The ultimate goal is *information*. You are looking for market statistics, guides, annual references, directories of industry participants, and other industry-specific information. Many resources provide business ratios by region or by comparable business size. Contact associations directly if possible, visit their websites to see what information is available.

Here are a few things you can do that will put you in direct contact with your customers to get first hand feedback about your idea.

- Focus groups gather a small group of people together for a discussion with an assigned leader about your product or service.

- Customer surveys may offer anonymous feedback
    o Existing customers
    o Potential customers

Step Five: Develop Your Business Plan

So now it's time to turn your great idea into a plan that will offer you a higher degree of comfort about spending your own money to underwrite the cost of start-up or convince others to invest. A business plan just outlines what you plan to do and how you plan to do it. Simply stated, a business plan conveys your business goals, the strategies you'll use to meet them, potential problems that may confront your business and ways to solve them, the organizational structure of your business (including titles and responsibilities), and finally, the amount of capital required to finance your venture and keep it going until it breaks even. The length of your business plan may vary based on the complexity of your great idea. The goal is clarity, specificity and a punch line than makes it marketable.

To keep it simple, a business plan usually contains three primary sections:

- **Your idea or concept.** This is where you describe your product or service, the impact you are trying to have on the industry and how you will be successful.

- **The target audience.** After all your homework is done, you are now equipped to narrow your focus on *who* will buy this product or service. This section of your plan describes these potential customers: who and where they are and what makes them buy. Here, you describe the competition and how you'll position yourself to beat it. This is also the section where you will describe in detail *how* you will operationalize your plan. This takes your plan from idea to production, marketing and distribution. Is this a one woman show or will you need additional employees to help you?

- **The money.** This section may require the help of an accountant. It requires a balance sheet, financial projections and how much money you will need to start and sustain your business over the next five years.

Step Six: Find Your First Customers

Plan done(check). Money in hand(check). Now who will be the first to buy your product or service? This is where you should choose wisely. Start with the target audience that will offer the highest probability of success. They will offer testimonials for future customers and create the foundation for future viability. And, it's okay to leverage family, friends and other personal or professional contacts. The goal is a successful start. You can increase the risk level of your market as your success ratio goes up.

Step Seven: Remain Optimistic and Realistic

Stepping out on your own to start a business is a scary venture. If you chose a business you are passionate about, it will help you remain optimistic about its success. However, if the stars do not align the first time, know when to pull out and be proud that you followed your dream. And ladies, dare to dream again.

Entrepreneurship is about living a few years of your life like most won't, so you can live the rest of your life like most can't.
—Anonymous

References:

Palmer, Kimberly. "Behind the 'Mompreneur' Myth"; *U.S. News and World Report.* 6/9/11.

SBA.Gov U.S. Small Business Administration (on-line resource)

WOMEN OF THE FUTURE:
THE NEW AGE LEADER

There was no respect for youth when I was young, and now that I am old, there is no respect for age - I missed it coming and going. —J.B. Priestly

I remember getting the call from the Human Resource Department to show up in Conference Room A for a meeting with the Image Consultant. I had just joined this organization and part of the on-boarding was to make sure all their consultants dressed appropriately for our clients throughout the country. Since consultants usually travel alone, how we present ourselves and represent the image of the company was critically important. The whole experience really made me pause. On some level I was even offended. Here I am, a seasoned executive representing organizations in a professional manner for more than three decades and at this point of my career I need an image consultant?

When I entered the room, there sat a young flamboyant man of about 25 years of age. His hair was spiked on the top of his head; and, he wore a bright colored shirt. As soon as I entered the room wearing a tailored suit with a muted colored shirt and comfortable pumps, he looked me up and down and asked me to sit in front of a floor length mirror. His first comment was "old school professional" and that with the exception of some tweaks here and there, my dress for the company would be fine. He advised me to consider wearing high-waist pants, dying my hair and wearing more make-up. Ugh.

Then he completely freaked me out! He started poofing and teasing my hair, saying I needed more height and volume. Now, ladies…you know messing with a woman's hair (especially a black woman's hair) is taboo unless you are at home or at the hair salon. And, if he was going for the same spiked look he touted…that was not happening! It took all my strength not to knock this crazy young man on his butt, but I had just gotten this job and didn't want to be fired because I decked the image consultant. At my age, I could write the book on dress for success and found the opinions of a *presumed* professional image consultant from another generation, fascinating.

I also wondered if the real impetus for the image consultant was *not* really coming from the dress from my generation, but the dress from the "new generation" leaders. You know…shorter skirts, lower cut tops, tighter pants and extreme make-up…the external presentation that can take an "old-school leader" like me over the edge. And, by the way, we still have most senior leaders who wear those "old school" shoes.

As I get older, I really am starting to feel like a Grandma in the workplace. My issues are starting to shift from those related to being a woman in leadership to the wide divide between my values, work style and even how I process information from the generations that have come after me. I am a "boomer" (born 1946- 1964) who struggles with the complete casual nature of Generation X, Y and beyond. I cannot tell you how many times I have gotten the comment about the hours that I put into work are "crazy". The future is a 9 am-5 pm workday. Most of our younger generation colleagues are not willing to "be like their mothers and fathers whose work ethic said it was okay to put in long hours". They don't want the stress.

This is the first time in American history that we have had *four* different generations working side-by-side in the workplace. I am old enough to remember when older workers were the bosses and younger workers did what was asked of them, no questions asked. There were definite rules as to how the boss was treated and how younger workers treated older workers. No longer: Roles today are all over the place and the rules are being rewritten daily.

At work, generational differences can affect everything, including recruiting, building teams, dealing with change, motivating, managing, and maintaining and increasing productivity. Think of how generational differences, relative to how people communicate, might affect misunderstandings, high employee turnover, difficulty in attracting employees and gaining employee commitment.

I get a big dose of the great generational divide at family functions. Those of like generations seem to group together to share their view of the world. Have you ever walked up on a conversation "out of your generation" and had no idea what they are talking about? This happens to me all the time, especially with the music they like and the words they use to describe things which seem to be a secret code I cannot understand. I am not sure when the English language got replaced, but I surely did not get the memo. Maybe it's a sign of my age that I find myself referring to "the good old days" and gravitating to the older crowd that I seem to relate to more. Even with family, communication can be a challenge trying to find common ground in an attempt to avoid controversy and conflict. What we care about is so different. Sometimes, even with my own grown children, I wonder who raised them. Now take that to the workplace…"*Houston, we have a problem*".

No matter what your age or gender, leading in this environment, means first understanding the differences exist and making sure you adapt "how you lead" to assure the greatest success across the generations. One size does not fit all! The following chart offers a snapshot into the different generations, work style and values. As with everything, this chart is not absolute for any one individual, but generalizations gleaned from research from a variety of authors. Behavior can be influenced by so many other variables. This should only be used as a frame of reference. Nothing replaces getting to know the people who work for you and what's important to them.

Traditionalists 1925-1945	Boomers 1946-1964	Xers 1965-1977	Millennials 1978 and after
Practical Always at work	Optimistic Want recognition	Skeptical	Hopeful and optimistic
Patient, loyal and hardworking Difficulty with change	Teamwork and cooperation Do not accept change	Self-reliant and techno literate Adaptable to change	Meaningful Work Moral mindset Social activism
Respectful of authority	Ambitious Physical health	Risk-taking	Value diversity and change
Rule followers Rewards later Prefer Structure	Workaholic –"Thank God Its' Monday"	Balance work and life	Technology savvy Immediate responsibility

So, how does a leader relate to these different individuals in the workplace? What are some best practices to consider? Here are some tips to add to your tool box.

Traditionalists
Remember:
➤ Majority of them have retired
➤ Possess intellectual capital and institutional knowledge
➤ Have strong work values and ethics
➤ Work is an obligation

➤ See themselves as vigorous, contributing members of the workforce
➤ Silent stoicism (not much feedback given or expected)

✓ Offer opportunities for them to mentor
✓ Offer opportunities to continue working
✓ Allow them to volunteer if they do not want to continue working
✓ Show them that you value their expertise and contribution

Baby Boomers

Remember:
➤ Invented and Value work-life balance
➤ *They are the leaders that are running our organizations today*
➤ Career oriented
➤ Work is an exciting adventure
➤ "Love the good life"
➤ Love job performance feedback

✓ Help them explore their next set of workplace options, and demonstrate how your organization can continue to use their talents.
✓ Walk the talk on work-life balance by redesigning their jobs to accommodate multiple life demands.
✓ Encourage them to enrich their present job and grow in place if they need to slow their career pace.

Xers

Remember:
➤ The next generation of leaders
➤ The most well educated generation

➢ Goal-oriented
➢ Work is a difficult challenge; a contract
➢ Free Agents vs. Company Loyalist
➢ Want to be challenged
➢ Led dot.com boom
➢ Want to have independence

✓ Talk to them about their reputation, not just job tasks; they want your candid perspective and feedback
✓ Acknowledge their ability to work independently and encourage them to leverage their entrepreneurial abilities.
✓ Help them get the most out of every job position by discussing what the job can do for them and what they can learn from it.

Millennials

Remember:
➢ Value independence
➢ Look for new challenges
➢ Challenge the status quo
➢ We're all in this together
➢ Want the opportunity to make an impact
➢ Work is a means to an end; fulfillment

✓ Demonstrate the stability and long-term value of your organization, and also show how your organization is flexible and filled with learning opportunities for them.
✓ Provide work schedules that help them build careers and families at the same time.
✓ Make groups and teams part of their job.

With the variety of points of view in the workplace, it's no wonder the controversy that can occur over a multitude of issues. For younger women currently holding or aspiring to fill leadership roles, they may not be open to the wisdom of the older generation. In some cases, they may not even see that a challenge exists. Recently, I had a young woman tell me, "There is no issue with diversity in the workplace". And in another breath wondered why another male co-worker got a job she felt she was more qualified for. If you are an Xer or Millennial reading this book, please leave yourself open to the value of mentorship. It's powerful and can facilitate much growth. You may not agree with all that is shared, but you may discover a gem or two that you will value for a lifetime.

The leadership characteristics favored by women give us a leg up in working across a variety of generations. Leverage those traits for success- people development, setting clear expectations and rewards, role modeling, inspirational leadership, and participative decision making. Men who continue to lead with an approach grounded in control may find themselves at odds with the new age workforce. And remember ladies, awareness and communication form the base for the secret sauce.

Each generation goes further than the generation preceding it because it stands on the shoulders of that generation. You will have opportunities beyond anything we've ever known.
—Ronald Reagan

References:

Lancaster, Lynne C.; Stillman, David. *When Generations Collide: Who They Are, Why They Clash, How to Solve the Generational Puzzle at Work.* HarperCollins Publishers Inc., 2002.

Sago, Brad. *"Uncommon Threads:* Mending the Generation Gap at Work," *Executive Update,* July 2000.

EXIT STAGE RIGHT—
KNOWING WHEN TO LEAVE

The World is running out of geniuses: Einstein died, Beethoven went deaf and I'm starting to have a migraine.
—Author Unknown.

During the interview process for any new job, most employers want to have some sense of your longevity. They want to know if they invest in you, will you stick around for at least five years. The process of constant rehire is stressful and costly. This is one place where I may offer different advice than most. I never give a timeframe for exit. I enter every job with the hope that it will offer me alignment with my personal/professional passion, continued growth and joy. If those three elements remain strong, then what reason do I have to leave?

The one thing we can always count on is constant change. In the workplace, leaders change, mergers and acquisitions happen and the economic landscape may change the whole direction or strategic priorities of the organization you signed on to. The alignment that was so visible to you in the beginning may be unidentifiable. For a leader, this misalignment creates stress and challenges your ability to support a vision you no longer believe in. Your effectiveness diminishes in achieving organizational results. And, no matter how much you think you hide this well of emotions and discontent, you become increasingly more transparent to those around you. Your non-verbals do not match the words that are coming out of your mouth. Let this be a warning to you that it may be time to exit stage right!

Most people who have made it to the ranks of leadership thrive in a work environment that promotes continuous growth and development. This does not have to equate to classes or specific training. It could mean a strong mentorship program that supports individual professional development. When continuous growth is a priority, organizations achieve amazing results, turnover rates are lower and employee engagement is high. For a leader, when the growing stops and they are in maintenance mode, they tend to become disinterested easily and flat. If this describes you, check to make sure you have availed yourself of all your job has to offer. Talk to your boss about growth possibilities. If none exist, it may be time to exit stage right!

Joy in the workplace is highly under-rated, especially for leaders. As children, we are constantly encouraged to strive for those top jobs at top pay. Rarely are we encouraged to choose jobs that bring us the greatest joy. Have you ever worked side by side with an employee that is miserable and unhappy in their job? It can plague an entire department. Their behavior can impact team work, which directly impacts the organization's ability to achieve results. If the leader is the miserable one, then multiply the impact three fold. If this describes you... then it may be time to exit stage right!

While you may want out when the economics of your company, or industry, are faltering, or a difficult merger or acquisition is in process, the most important reason to consider a change is when you stop loving what you do. So, why do we stay? Pay and security are driving forces. In this economy, think smart. If you are seeing the warning signs described previously, start to plot your next move. Unless you are in a situation that requires intervention by your Human Resources Department, research your options and strategically make a decision about the next step in your career. A bird in hand is always better in today's economic climate than none at all. Try to find small things that bring you joy everyday while you create a transition to a better match.

If you do find yourself in a situation that compromises your integrity, you may have to leave and have faith that a different bird will fill your hand. Exit stage right!

But I am fearful of taking such a dramatic step. Fear of the unknown can paralyze you even though you know it's the right thing to do. We have all kinds of conversations in our head. For example:

"Will I be able to find another comparable job?" For women leaders who have struggled long and hard to reach their current positions, this is a hard hitting reality. Executive roles continue to be male dominant in most industries. Some organizations still feel they are "taking a risk" on hiring a female into certain leadership roles. Once you have made it, you wonder with each new job if you will be able to get past these road blocks again. Just once you would like to be judged on your credentials instead of your exterior presentation first. You even wonder if you have the stamina to run the gauntlet.

What will my friends and colleagues think? Women have an enormous sense of pride when they reach leadership status, especially if they have broken through long standing glass or even concrete ceilings. Leaving those positions for reasons other than for a promotion, relocation or maybe having a child can often create a buzz among friends and colleagues about "why". Some may think you are wimping out or don't have what it takes to do the job. Others cannot believe you are walking away from the prestige and lucrative salary few achieve. You may also have seen yourself as a role model and believe walking away sends the wrong message to those who have looked up to you.

I certainly understand and do not want to minimize the realities of making a decision to leave a job you have worked so hard to achieve. It is emotionally gut wrenching. But, you deserve more for yourself and your well-being. Having faith in your abilities, reframing the possibilities for your future and being courageous will set the stage for your future success. Other doors will open for you. Fear can blind you to what might be right in front of you. These messages are even more powerful for our women leaders of tomorrow who will someday face these same challenges.

And what if I am just burned out! Are you feeling tired all the time? Irritated easily? Are you experiencing long periods of disinterest? Do problems seem insurmountable and does your future seem bleak? You may be the victim of burnout. Burnout reduces your productivity and saps your energy, leaving you feeling increasingly helpless, hopeless, cynical, and resentful. Eventually, you may feel like you have nothing more to give. Being burned out means feeling empty,devoid of motivation, and beyond caring. Burnout can also cause long-term changes to your body that make you vulnerable to illnesses like colds and flu. Because of its many consequences, it's important to deal with burnout right away. This is different than occasional periods of high stress. Stressed people can still imagine that if they can just get everything under control, they'll feel better.

The first step in healing burnout is to be able to recognize the symptoms in yourself or have a safe friend or colleague to give you honest feedback. Step two is to stop being victim and change your current state. Burnout may be an early warning for an exit plan or just an end product of a period of intense focus or stress. This could be on a personal or professional level. Please note: you cannot separate the two. We all bring home to work and work to home. It's how we deal with them in the alternate universe that makes a difference. Look for ways to better manage your stress or seek professional support. Step three is to build up your internal bank account by taking better care of your physical and emotional health. Step four would be if all the previous steps fail…exit stage right! Your well-being is an essential ingredient to being a great leader.

Possible remedies for burnout include:

- Take a deep breath and slow down. Cut back whatever commitments and activities you can. Give yourself time to rest, reflect, and heal.

- Get support from family, friends and colleagues. When we are burned out, we naturally want to separate from others. Wrong strategy. We need nurturing to heal. Sometimes just openly sharing your feelings with those who love you can begin to relieve some of the pressure. You do not have to face the world alone.

- Re-evaluate your personal priorities and goals. Is this really where you want to be? Are you neglecting something that is really important to you? How can you shift back to those things that bring you joy? This may be a great time to re-evaluate your job description for clarity of roles and responsibilities. Has your current job morphed into something you did not sign up for?

- Exercise and eat right. And, get that body moving! Those elevated endorphins really do work as mood changers. ZUMBA is a wonderful full body workout. If it doesn't kill you, you will feel wonderful and burn almost 700 calories an hour!

- Take a proactive rather than reactive approach to addressing challenges. Make sure you take your conversations to the right person. Being part of a rumor mill does not help your cause. Most people are responsive to a respectful approach, even if they do not agree with you. Take your concerns directly to the source as appropriate. It may even be helpful to rehearse with a friend or colleague your key discussion points so that you do not lead with your emotions. Even if you do not walk away with the answer you were looking for, you should feel great about standing up for yourself and taking the opportunity to be heard.

- Try something new! This can be at home or at work. Discuss options with your boss. It may be that a new location or job within the current organization may just do the trick.

- Take a vacation. Even a small trip can get you back on track… if you turn off all access to work or your source of stress. This includes our obsession with technology and all things that start with an "I" (phones, pads…).

The world of work is rapidly changing. It is logical that the average person could hold 15 -20 different jobs in their lifetime. This is particularly relevant as the age of retirement gets closer to 70 years. So, don't panic if you must leave your job. We are past the era when people only have one to three jobs in their career. If you can, start planning for a change while you're happy in your current job. Take advantage of all the opportunities you're given to develop new skills, network with other people, and develop a support system so that if you do leave, you'll land on your feet.

Please remember to leave your organization with grace and style. You never know when you will need or meet these same individuals again. Our professional circles are not as big as we think they are.

Never burn your bridges. The sparks will hit you in the ass.
—Judith Luther-Wilder,
    cofounder and co-CEO of Women Inc.

SHEROES AMONG US

Sheroes. As necessary as water.
Sheroes. As beautiful as the morning sun.
Sheroes. As sweet as rain.
Sheroes. The word.
Makes you smile rivers.
—Sonia Sanchez

When you think of sheroes, what names come to mind...? Harriet Tubman (the original American freedom rider), Mother Theresa, Coretta Scott King, Michele Obama, Hillary Clinton, Marian Wright Edelman or Olympic champion speed racer Bonnie Blair?

They are real women who inspire us to reach beyond where we ever thought we could go. They give us courage and lift our spirits. They are all races and colors of the rainbow hailing from all over the world. Many have looked fear directly in the eye and many have suffered unimaginable pain in order to change the world for others. Their actions have touched thousands or the heart of one. Their struggles for good give us hope and remind us of the power of human goodness.

Just look at the power of our First Lady, Michele Obama. On a regular basis she graces the covers of magazines, newspapers and our television screen. Many anxiously wait to see what she will wear to the next White House affair and runs to buy copies...seeking to experience for just one moment what it would feel like to live in her shoes. As the first African American First Lady, her words and actions will offer young women everywhere the hope of what they can be. Michele Obama is the ultimate Shero of our recent times.

Most of us admire sheroes from afar and usually see them far away from our everyday reality...but sheroes are among us. Sheroes stand next to us at the water cooler and sit next to us in church. They do not have to appear in the news or history books, but in our hearts and minds for the smallest act that makes a difference...even if it is just to us. They can be family, friends or a stranger who is completely unaware of your admiration. No one shero is completely like another, even though they may share some common attributes we yearn to emulate.

All my sheroes have shown tremendous courage against adversity and have maintained a sense of integrity throughout it all. Their strength is palpable and inspires me during times when I question my own inner strength. Their names never made the evening news, but are those women who have gained success in their lives by hard work, honesty and perseverance and not selling their souls to the devil or literally lying on their backs to get ahead. I can close my eyes and see the faces of former managers, peers and family members including the face of my Mom. I hear their stories of pain and triumph. I can hear them telling me to continue my journey and be that shero to someone else.

Sheroes We Share

Elizabeth Blackwell *(1849)*
First woman to earn a medical degree.

Belva Ann Lockwood *(1879)*
First woman to practice law before U.S Supreme Court

Gail Collins *(2001)*
Head New York Times *Editorial Board*

Ann Dunwoody *(2008)*
First four-star general

Michele Obama *(2010-present)*
First African American First Lady of the United States

I asked a few friends to share their stories about sheroes in their life. This is what they had to say.

Grandma: Carla's Shero

I was only 6 years old when my father died. Because my mother needed to work full-time after his death, whenever I was sick or had a day off from school, I went to my grandmother's house. My grandmother was born in 1896 and she graduated from "The Sheboygan College of Business" in 1914, which was then the equivalent of having a college education. She literally married "the boy next door." She had a full-time job as an office worker at a furniture factory and every night my grandfather would wait for her outside her building so he could walk her home. At first she wasn't interested and tried to find ways to avoid him, but after a while she came to realize that she liked walking with him and she chose to walk through life with him.

During the Depression my grandmother fed the "tramps and hobos" whenever they came asking for food. She gave these homeless strangers whatever she could, because, "well, they were hungry and someone needed to help them, didn't they?" She also sold baked goods out of her back door to make extra money during this time, and she was a wonderful baker! When I was growing up, she taught me how to bake, and to this day, when I use her recipes, people compliment me on my cooking. Her recipes, though, could be a challenge; they'd say things like: two handsful of flour, 15 cents worth of walnuts, add enough milk to make a soft dough, stir until it feels "right," and bake in a hot oven until it is done.

Grandma also taught me how to knit, crochet, embroider, and play a mean game of canasta.

When I was very young, my grandfather had a serious stroke and was completely paralyzed on one side of his body. My grandmother took care of him, night and day, while he lay in a hospital bed in their extra bedroom. As far as I know, he never, ever, got out of that bed and she fed him, bathed him, turned him, dressed him, and cared for all of his needs every day for 5 years. I never heard a complaint from her.

But mostly, when I remember Grandma, I remember the fun we had. We laughed, played cards, watched TV game shows all afternoon, and sat up 'way past my bedtime to watch the news and Johnny Carson. When I was old enough, I'd drive Grandma to her doctor's appointments and take her shopping, always making a day of it by stopping somewhere to have lunch.

She was smart, educated, hard working, well-read, funny, kind, generous, and just the most wonderful grandmother anyone could have. She loved me. She was, and always will be, everything I hope I can be. My grandmother, Marie Winkle is my shero.

Submitted by Carla Wiggins

Miss Harriett Starr Mason
Teacher and Headmistress of Mason
Preparatory School, Charleston, SC

"Books are our friends." Miss Mason said as she opened the cover to the new book she planned to read aloud to us. We were the children in the first grade; all seated on the carpeted floor, eagerly waiting for Miss Mason to begin the day's reading time. Miss Mason loved to read, and I loved to listen to her read. She read books about adventure, people who lived in different times, in different places, with different dreams and goals. One time she read about a Native American child who lived in the Rocky Mountains; another time we learned about the "Swamp Fox," an American Revolutionary war hero from our own State of South Carolina.

"Books are our friends," Miss Mason said. She looked at us directly to see if we were ready for her to begin reading aloud. Her eyes twinkled when she was pleased. They narrowed when she was not happy with us.

I preferred the twinkle. Her hair was short and brown, peppered with gray. She tended to wear earth toned suits. I remember tweed.

"Books are our friends," Miss Mason said. She told us that books are there when we want them to be, and they will be there for us to read anytime we want. Books are constant; they are steady companions. They tell us about people we might want to try to be like, or not be like. They acquaint us with places we may want to visit or live someday. They explain courage; they describe fear; they create laughter; they give details about the triumph of the human spirit. They show us what we can dream to become.

Miss Mason simply opened the world of possibilities to me through her love of reading. I could picture myself as a Native American girl who lived in a tepee and hunted buffalo. I could envision myself as a Patriot who helped America earn its independence. I could imagine that I might become anything I had the potential to be. And, Miss Mason encouraged that kind of thinking. She did not just tell me I could become what I dreamed to be; she believed that I could. She believed in me.

Submitted By: Leigh Walter Cellucci, Ph.D.

Lathran Presents: Shirley Johnson - Humanitarian

I would like to take this opportunity to tell you of a great humanitarian. A humanitarian whose contributions will never truly be acknowledged by our society. This humanitarian is my sister-in-law, Shirley Canzater Johnson. Shirley was born April 6, 1951. She was the second of five children born to Emma and Odell Canzater. Shirley attended C.A. Johnson High School where she met her future husband and my brother, George Earl Johnson. They graduated in 1969 and wedded in April 1974. Shirley's humanitarianism was exhibited through giving of herself and her possessions always with a smile.

I remember Shirley giving food to someone she had never seen before. An older woman whom some would refer from her appearance as a "bag lady" was walking down the street in front of Shirley's house. Shirley was on the porch watering her plants at the time. The lady stopped and talked with Shirley. Shirley offered her some food, and gave her some dry goods to take home. I am not sure how this part came to be, but Shirley would leave a grocer bag of food on her front porch for the lady every week. I know about this situation not because Shirley told anyone what she was doing, but because my brother told me.

Shirley would give of herself to children she came in contact with. Biologically, Shirley had one child, although she was the mother to many children. She is known for taking in children who did not want to stay in their homes because of neglect or loneliness. Shirley also acts as mother and close friend to the children in the family. Shirley's place was the hang out for big children and little children. She was always in the Kitchen cooking for somebody.

Shirley was charitable in giving of her time. She would never say no to running errands for anyone who asked. Even when she was ill, she was willing to give of herself to help someone else. When she could no longer drive, she would still say yes to babysitting.

I said earlier that society will never truly acknowledge this great humanitarian, Shirley's kindness will never be rewarded by this society because on March 24, 1999, Shirley died. She is no longer around to give out those acts of kindness. But the lives she touched are changed forever.

Submitted By Lathran Woodard, Executive Director,
South Carolina Primary Care Association

Thoughts From Nancy

I struggle with the question about who is my shero. So many women come to mind...my grandmother who didn't know how babies were born with her first pregnancy and then she later became a mid-wife and opened her own restaurant, my aunt who left a bad marriage with an alcoholic and went to the big city of Fargo to pursue her dreams even though the family frowned on her decision or my mom who taught me that it didn't matter if those you supervise like you so long as you are fair they will respect you. So I will continue to refine my thoughts but it has been great to think about how brave these women were in much more challenging times than today. They give me strength to find my dream.

Submitted by Nancy Erckenbrach

Renee's Keys To Success

Making it to the top, achieving your goals, reaching that brass ring, is the best way to describe how I feel about the many women of leadership who open doors, windows, and pathways to your personal and professional success. As an African American female of 54, a product of a single mother with six children to clothe and feed, my journey to success had many helping hands of support which carried me through decisions of quality education and personal discipline.

These are the two key characteristics that the many women of leadership instilled in me during years of growth and development. "You must get your degree – not just a B.A. – a master's degree!" – words from my first female manager, who was a very polished and accomplished professional. She was tall and slender, with style and grace. I admired how she maintained not only her appearance but also her intellect. She was a smart cookie! I loved working for her because she stood up for her staff, no matter what. I clearly have adapted her ability to support my staff, and I continue to aspire to achieve her style and intellect.

Discipline is another key principle instilled in me from women who had achieved professional and social status in their fields of leadership. "You must read more, learn more, do more, and do it better!" These are words which encircled my brain through many hours of study and working my way through college. Not many hours left for school when you work from 2 to 10 p.m., five days a week! Discipline is what got me through, and understanding how to manage my day by managing all that I had to do through lists of activities. This is still how I function today, I map out months at a time, with a clear focus in knowing all the activities which are essential for me to complete.

Submitted by Renee Frazier

I want to personally thank all my friends for sharing their stories about their sheroes. Take a moment to remember those special women who have touched your lives and offered you a promise for the future. Then pass on the favor to someone else. Be a shero.

—Jackie

IN SEARCH OF BALANCE

Life is 10 percent what you make it, and 90 percent how you take it." —Irving Berlin

The poet and author Maya Angelou describes us as *Phenomenal Women* with inner mysteries that make us unique. Who knew having a uterus would give us so much power? But when you stop and think about it, none of us would have developed into anything... without the touch of a woman. Yet most of us are too tired assuming the multitude of societal roles we play, we don't have the energy to appreciate how special we really are.

Most women today hold down jobs and work more than 40 hours per week, while juggling family and taking care of the home. If you are in a leadership position....add another set of variables to the equation and double the hours worked per week. There are some researchers who say, women are genetically wired to be superior at multitasking. They describe us as "peripheral visionaries", able to follow several trains of thought simultaneously. Men, by contrast, seem more capable of focusing intensely on single topics. So you see ladies, we just can't help ourselves...it's in our genes to handle all this craziness.

Our flaw is often the inability to *take care* of ourselves. We often lose ourselves (mind, body and spirit) in the busyness of our lives...in all the roles....in all the tasks. Balance is not a priority...we will get to it...if we can. But...can we really afford to put ourselves on the back burner? What's at stake if we just let ourselves go?

The headlines are full of stories about the rise of illness in women: depression, heart disease, cancer, obesity, musculoskeletal disorders and stress. Many factors contribute to stress among women, including: job conditions (heavy workload, little control over work, role ambiguity and conflict, job insecurity, sexual harassment) combined with work and family balance issues. This stress leads to cardiovascular disease, musculoskeletal disease, depression and burnout...we eat more... and the cycle continues.

One researcher in a *Web MD Medical News* article (November 15, 2005) entitled *Women More Sensitive to Stress than Men* states:

"Serious disorders such as major depression, anxiety, and autoimmune dysfunctions, all linked to higher levels of circulating glucocorticoids (stress hormones), are more prevalent among women than men" James Herman, PhD, professor and stress neurobiologist at the University of Cincinnati

Now our hormones are driving the bus!

What's compelling women to take on the world? Jane Appelgate in the book *On Our Own Terms* offers her opinion about what drives women leaders stating: "Women who go into business or manage large companies are obsessed with succeeding because so many people are watching and so much is at risk. We risk alienating our families because our business becomes a demanding baby. We risk losing our romantic relationships because our boyfriends and husbands resent our success. We risk losing our friends because they are angry they never see us anymore. Because so much is at risk-emotionally, financially and spiritually-we work even harder to succeed".

The decline of our economy, the cost of housing, as well as our desire to have all the toys, cars, flat screen TV's that eat up our living spaces...also drives us to work more...either to survive or just have the things we think we need. It takes both parents working or increased financial resources to meet those demands.

Over the past 20 years, the demands of the modern workplace are perceived to have impacted heavily on family and community life. There's less time for volunteering. Mothers wish they had more time with their children. "Me time" seems to be shrinking and an aging population means eldercare is becoming a serious issue, often a responsibility assumed by the females in the family. And the sad news is that many folks think they have no choice.

In 2008, The Studer Group conducted a Work/Life Blend study (Studer, 2009) that focused on how the healthcare industry is meeting the needs of women. 8000 women who work in healthcare participated in the study. The results may not surprise you:

> *"Only 47% of the women surveyed were satisfied with their current work-life balance.*
> *45% of the respondents experienced a work-family conflict at least one day or more per week including non-day shift work, mandatory overtime, having children under the age of 18, and having responsibilities for the care of other dependent relatives.*
> *The strongest correlation with work satisfaction was the perception of supervisor support.*
> *Women are looking for employer-sponsored options to help them balance work and life, with concierge services and flexible hours receiving the highest preferred options."*

We all have the power to make choices in our lives. Begin to make some choices that put you first! Take back your life! Remember, there is no magic pill and each person's journey to a balanced life is personal. However, there are numerous approaches or strategies you can try… the first step is realizing you are out of balance. Running is not healthy and should not be the norm.

Your To Do List to a Balanced Life

Recognize the need for balance and commit to addressing it in your life.
If you just devote all your time to work, then you're going to be neglecting the social, spiritual and a multitude of other important aspects of your life…be a whole person…be fulfilled in all different aspects of your life.

Figure out what works for you.
The "right balance" is a very personal thing and will change for each person at different times in their lives. There is no "one size fit all". What we need as a young adult is very different from what we need in our senior years…it also may be very different based on our culture,

our gender or any variety of factors. The point is…it is unique for each of us, but definitely something that we all require in our lives.

Beware of the technology chains that bind.

Cell phones and PC's blur the distinction between work and personal time…don't fall victim to this temptation.

Use your faith to help put life into perspective.

Faith makes all things possible. It offers me a healthy way to balance all personal, interpersonal, work related and community responsibilities. It is a rock to stand on in this crazy world…strength.

Be organized.

The most important issues related to having a good balance are organization, planning and time management. This could mean planning meals a week in advance, laying out clothes the night before and spending as much evening time with young children as possible.

Recognize that balance takes work.

Balance is a necessary part of life. It's up to you to manage it. The choices made have costs and benefits associated with them. It is something that always has to be kept in mind to ensure that no component is neglected for too long.

Here are some choices to think about:

- Consciously separate work and home.
- Consciously put family first
- Work less hours
- Choose shift work so one partner is home to care for other family members
- Learn to make do with less
- Decide to postpone or not have children
- Postpone major career moves to accommodate personal life goals that are not related to work

These are all within our control…we may not like the choice…but it is ours to make.

Have goals.

Know your goal and plan accordingly. Know your priority in life and what's important.

Don't sweat the small stuff.

I don't stress out about daily life situations and I remember how fortunate I am to be healthy and safe. Most of all, you only live once and you need to strive for what you want and make the best of it. I don't want to regret anything I didn't do now when I am older.

Enjoy life-focus on what is going well, not what is stressful.

Take time to play, laugh, love, work, cry together and respect each other. We all make mistakes at home and work. Take time for yourself and smile.

Find a job you enjoy.

We spend more waking hours at work then we do with loved ones. It's imperative to be in an environment that brings you joy. How miserable to spend most of your waking hours unhappy and stressed out.

Remain fit and use exercise as a way to deal with stress.

I feel people who exercise regularly are better able to handle stress. Whether it's 5 a.m. or 6 in the evening, exercising can improve the quality of your day. I also believe in recognizing the need for leisure activities that you enjoy, feeling connected to the community, and having goals for the future.

Make a date with yourself.

Many of you have probably heard about this trend for married couples to have a date night actually scheduled. Don't misunderstand; I am not knocking this trend. Having balance includes quality time with the important folks in your life no matter how you get it. But I would like to push you into starting a new trend-date night, morning...lunch...weekend....with yourself. If scheduling works best for you (which I do), go for it! During your date time do whatever it is that makes you happy...exercise, read, meditate, pray, shop, get a massage....whatever gives you just a small break for yourself. You will be surprised the change you immediately start to feel in the quality of your life.

You can even start small, blocking out 15 minutes or 30 minutes a day.

I can tell you that in the beginning, family members, friends and co-workers will not understand. My family makes jokes about Jackie time, but occasionally will ask me to take it because it significantly changes my mood and interactions with them. I really believe I am a better leader, when I take the time for me to get balanced and I already know my health in general has improved.

I have made a conscious commitment to my future and the quality of that future. I want to be there to see my grandsons graduate from college. I want to take long walks with my husband during our retirement years. I want to be able to find Jackie (all of me--mind, heart, body and spirit) when I look back on my life in review. This is a daily commitment and the journey has not been an easy one. It's so easy to get lost in the daily madness and the busyness of our lives, to make excuses and feel real comfortable multi-tasking.

Remember, there is no magic pill to finding balance. Each of you has to spark that journey in yourself or continue on the cycle of madness. Finding balance has to be a priority. Remember, there is no future without us as healthy, contributing, phenomenal women!

> *"Balance is the perfect state of still water. Let that be our model. It remains quiet within and is not disturbed on the surface."* —Confucius

References:

Enkelis, Liane, Olsen, Karen, Lewinstein, Marion; *On Our Own Terms* (1995) Berrett-Kohler Publishers.

Studer, Quint; Health Care Strategy Alert (2009) Issue 1; *Creating Great Places for Women to Work*; Forum for Health Care Strategies.

LETTERS TO OUR MOM

*If your actions inspire others to dream more, learn more,
do more and become more, you are a leader.*
—John Quincy Adams

Two significant contributions I have made to this world are my beautiful daughters, Jennifer and Kimberley. I have watched them grow into women discovering all that life has to offer. Their journey has not always been easy. Sometimes they have experienced the same bumps along the way that I have, including the continuing barriers for women to advance in the workplace. Even though we have made some strides, the struggle continues. As mothers to future leaders, we need to continue to offer them the wisdom and inner strength for success. It is a precious gift. To our boys, we need to offer them a new lens to see the world-through which the blending of unique characteristics all individuals bring to the table is more powerful than any one individual or gender can offer alone. To our girls, we much teach them to have pride in their femininity. Gender should not define power, expertise or how far they can progress up the corporate ladder. Our children are the key to changing the current realities in the workforce for men and women. There will come a day when it's ok to wear a yellow suit!

Grandsons Christian and Darian

Dear Mommy,

These kids are getting on my nerves! Darian needs me for this, Christian is crying for that, and to top it off my Husband is on his way home from work and I haven't even begun dinner!   I have a job interview tomorrow, I have not thought about what I am going to wear, let alone what I will do with my hair if I have any by the end of this day.

I say to myself, "Breathe Kimberley you have seen your mother do this time and time again." So I am breathing and taking a much needed break and I find myself feeling better. As I am sitting here acquiring more strength, I can only think to thank you. How would I have ever known how to handle stress? How to be a great mother? How to be a loving wife? How to be a successful woman?

You have taught me that no matter what and how much I am going through, a woman can be strong too. A woman is reliable. A woman is a nurturer, and a woman can be a fighter as well. I always wondered how you did it. I used to say to myself, "I can never be a woman like my mother". But after my day today, I am starting to realize I am my mother's child. I am just as strong as you are.

Your unconditional love throughout the trials and tribulations of my life has helped to mentor me into the woman I am, and the mother that I strive to be. For this and so much more, I want to thank you.

So what do I wear tomorrow? When I spoke to the gentleman from GBMC, he said they want a professional multi-tasker with the ability to manage chaos in a stressful environment. I thought to myself, "You obviously don't know me or my life." Anyway, I thought about these black slacks, with a black and white shirt. Then I remembered the guy saying that there were a lot of interviews that day for this same position. I think I will tune into my inner Jackie, and stick with the black slacks, but maybe pair it with this cute bright pink button down shirt.

Ok Mom, I have got to go, these kids are running wild, and my Husband should be here any minute. I hope he wants chicken because that's what is on the menu tonight. I think I will use one of your recipes. Oh yeah, thank you for making me the cook that I am!

I love you Mommy. I hope to see you soon!

Your baby girl, Kim

Mom,

I can't begin to count the number of times that I've heard someone say to me, "you are just like your mother." It is easy to see some of our physical similarities: the sloping of our noses, the freckles scattered on our cheeks, the curliness of our hair, our height. We even sound similar when we speak. So much so that even Grandma has mistaken us on the telephone. However, it wasn't until the day of your twentieth wedding anniversary, as I sat in the University of Maryland cafeteria that I realized just how similar my life was to yours. I was the same age, at

Jennifer on a medical mission in Ecuador

the same school and about to embark on the same career path that you had chosen just twenty years prior.

For as long as I can recall, I knew that I wanted to become a nurse. As a child, I didn't know the scope of a nurse's practice or the potential for growth in that career field. I just knew they cared for the sick, so that was what I wanted to do. I watched and learned as you maneuvered through your nursing career, advancing from a staff nurse, to charge nurse, to nurse manager and to nurse practitioner. I also observed you later take on the roles of educator, lobbyist, grant writer, consultant, coach and executive. You allowed me to see, through your experiences, what opportunities may be available to me in the future.

That's why it should come as no surprise that like you, I accepted a position at the Johns Hopkins Hospital after graduation. It's funny how even though we chose to work in different areas, you on an inpatient unit and me in the operating room, we both specialized in gynecology. Even my career advancement over the last eleven years has closely mimicked yours: from staff nurse, to charge nurse, to surgical service coordinator, to shift coordinator and to my current position as a practice administrator.

It amazes me how you were able to do all of this at such a young age, especially while raising two small children. There were so many times that I thought the stress of working full time while pursuing dual degrees in graduate school, yet another one of our similarities, would KILL me! And I didn't even have the added responsibilities that come with being a mom & wife. You've sacrificed so much in an effort to provide the best life possible for your family. This even meant that at times, you had to bring me and Kimmie along with you while you studied or worked.

I am very grateful that you are my mom because you have been such an inspiration in my life and in the lives of others. You have a tremendous amount of drive, ambition, spirit, character and love. I really hope that we are similar in this respect too. I make very few major decisions in my personal or professional life without turning to you first for advice. You have mentored me on how to be an effective leader, a compassionate nurse and a strong, confident woman. When the time comes, I only hope that I will be a great mother and wife like you. So the next time someone says, "you are just like your mother," I will smile with pride and simply say "Thank you."

Thank you Mom for your continued guidance, support and love!
I love you,
Jenni

My beautiful daughters- Jennifer and Kimberly.

With every deed you are sowing a seed, though the harvest you may not see. —Ella Wheeler Wilcox

There are two lasting bequests we can give our children: One is roots. The other is wings. —Hodding Carter, Jr.

WEARING THE YELLOW SUIT:
KEY TAKE-AWAYS

*"There is nothing more difficult to take in hand, more peril-
ous to conduct, or more uncertain in its success, than to take
the lead in the introduction of a new order of things."*
—Niccolo Machiavelli

It's a brand new day! Bridging the gender gap in leadership will be an essential ingredient for success in business across multiple industries. Here are the facts:

- Women now earn 58% of all college degrees
    - 60% of all master's degrees
    - 49% of all medical degrees
    - 48% of all law degrees
    - 30% of all math PhD's

- 40% of women are the primary breadwinners in households across the country

- 15 Fortune 500 companies are headed by women

- There are 10.1 million women owned businesses in the U.S.

The landscape is rapidly changing. Success in business can longer be driven by the same tactics and leadership dynamics of the past. Soon, the balance of dominance in the workforce may actually shift the other way and women will need to be heard. And, it doesn't have to be a tug of war for power. It's not about who wears the pants or the *yellow suit*.

It's about building a leadership and workforce that values the best that both have to offer. The unique characteristics and talents of both sexes are much more powerful together than any one individual standing alone or with others who are all the same. Blending can maximize the potential of individuals and will give an organization a competitive edge. It will also help an organization be more responsive to diverse communities and customers.

This will not be an easy journey. It's very difficult to change behaviors that have been a part of us since the era of cave men and women. Cave men with clubs in hand and aggressive sounds would battle to gain control of their pack. Aggression was equated with strength and having more often got you the role as leader with more privileges and prestige. This rank was never held by a woman who was perceived too weak to lead. This snapshot of history does not have to be our future. It will take courage and persistence grounded in shared values for making a difference for those following in our footsteps. When I look back 10 years from now, I hope we have evolved to a point where it's ok to wear a yellow suit! Getting rid of the hosiery requirement in summer wouldn't be bad either.

Key Take-Aways:

- Women should feel proud of the attributes they bring to any organization. Our touch is unique and doesn't have to be masked or perceived as a sign of weakness. We just need to believe in our own inner strength. We are effective leaders being fully who we are…leading our way.

- Real change must transcend the "number" of women in the top jobs and address the reasons why there are barriers in the first place. Those barriers will continue to prevent the success of even one who has been allowed to join the ranks of their male counterparts.

- Diversity is a collective mixture of individuals, cultures and organizational expertise. It is much more than skin color, gender, or background. It's internal and external.

- Leaders in any industry are primarily white males, images further accentuated in the media. These images and their underlying messages become integrated into how we define ourselves and others. They can also limit who we think we can become further accentuating the divide between the sexes.

- Girls and boys differ profoundly in how they hear, how they see, how they respond to stress --and those differences are present at birth. These are not negative attributes, just differences. Society has placed values on them, not our genes.

- Women do not need to trade in their own personal style as long as it takes into consideration the professional demeanor of the role, the audience and overall corporate culture (i.e., formal or business casual). It may even prove to uplift the organizational mood that is often depressed devoid of color and an appreciation for differences.

- Stepping into the "real you" can be freeing and enhance your effectiveness in any role including the top job. Sure, it may upset the apple cart or challenge the norm, but don't let that stop you. Be confident in your abilities. Ultimately, organizational results, primarily money, is valued more than what you wear.

- The numerous roles women assume daily are a part of our make-up and influence how we interact with the workplace. They cannot be separated when talking about diversity or the advancement of women of any ethnicity in leadership. For women leaders…success in business means we have to find the way to balance all these roles.

- 92% of jobs are about using the employees' intelligence, instincts and ideas to create great outcomes. The human capital no longer resides in just the hands, but now within the head and heart of the workforce. A nurturing leader can unlock that human potential in an organization and take it to a whole different level. Nurturing is a key attribute women leaders bring to an organization.

- The experiences of women who use sex and manipulation to advance their careers may not achieve the anticipated outcomes. If they indeed make it to the top job, it may be a short lived victory.

- Except for the rare cases in which excess weight makes it impossible for a person to perform a job, overweight individuals deserve the same access to employment possibilities as do thin people and deserve to earn as much for their work. All big-boned women are not un-healthy and a risk for employers. *Size should not be used an immediate indicator of capability to do a job or to be a leader.* This type of thinking is totally unacceptable.

- Even if the same degree of research validation does not exist on this topic as with other forms of discrimination, tall women most certainly have felt the wrath or ill will of short men in the workplace. There is also little or no discussion about height as the underlying cause of the discourse. It's one of our more silent forms of discrimination where *size does matter.*

- There is no written rule that the man needs to make the most money. This is an old value that needs to fade. *Wallet size should not matter* (unless it's completely empty). Men can stay home with the children and not lose their masculinity. No matter how far we think we have come, we still have some cultural growth in this area.

- The informal and professional bond between women, no matter what race, in a business setting can be powerful and should be encouraged. It doesn't mean we are setting up a male versus female workplace. It means, woman understand the needs and challenges of other women and are in the best position to advise, teach and nurture growth and development. It does not mean, because we are "sisters", we are obliged to give a fellow sister jobs or advancement, not deserved or earned.

- The secret to creating a high quality, high performance work team is the ability to use the strengths of each team member and the blending of their different viewpoints, personalities, cultures, processes, procedures, and operations into a tight, cohesive team that has bonded by overcoming shared adversity. The leader must take the time and put forth the effort to truly understand all of the individuals that make up the team. Men need to understand the strengths of females on their team and the same of female leaders about men. Each attribute should be valued to move the organization forward.

- Women enter the workforce and leadership roles at different points in their life cycle. Different than our male counterparts, we are often judged or valued as of reflection of that part of our journey. The truth is that it should not determine our ability to lead. How we manage these different stops along the way- single, married, with children, graduate education…is ours to manage. The employer can and should be sensitive to the varied needs of women, but not judge their success on an unexplored variable.

- Maintain a focus on your personal relationships and never stop talking to your partners. Even through rough days, find a time to find solace in each other. There is some truth in the old saying, "never go to bed angry with your partner". But, if your relationship was lousy before the job, don't expect miracles after you start working or step into those leader shoes. The job itself may not be the cause of your discourse, but it may take you over the top.

- Remember, the first step learning how to dance with one another in the workplace is to understand how the other person thinks, what they value and being open to their point of view. We don't have to always like or even adopt the "male perspective", just as they do not have to accept a "woman's perspective". But, if we take the time to understand and really *hear* each other, we go a long way to finding the common ground for success.

- Five main components to transformational leadership: charisma, inspiration, intellectual stimulation, individualized consideration, and extra effort. In the past, leadership qualities have traditionally been viewed as more masculine than feminine. However, the attributes of transformational leaders are more aligned with the attributes often considered female. The value placed on the caring and nurturing of the workforce has dramatically increased over aggression.

- Effective, leaders must display a balance of feminine and masculine behaviors. If these behaviors cannot be found in one individual, they must be present in a cohesive leadership team, giving credence to the value of blending in achieving organizational excellence.

- The ultimate objective of diversity is to create a high performance organization including competent, self-motivated employees and an inclusive leadership support system. Diversity must be viewed as *central* to that objective and not a separate initiative or program.

- Leading inclusion requires a personal commitment (transformation), modeling inclusive behaviors, and influencing others (through accountability) to behave and produce results consistent with a culturally competent way of thinking.

- Assimilation is not required...professionalism is the key.

- Mentors can help women leaders navigate corporate waters and cultural norms. They also offer a safe place to vent frustrations and work through challenges as a woman executive.

- Mentors can play a significant role in the successful on-boarding of new female executives.

- Affinity groups help increase employee retention by reducing the social isolation of being the only "one" within a department or division. A good employee affinity group can also boost diversity among a company's new hires. That's because under-represented employees are more likely to refer friends to their employer when they know that an infrastructure exists to support and utilize them effectively.

- Explicit diversity and inclusion indicators allow organizations to monitor their progress and define priorities for action. It is highly recommended that organizations use a variety of indicators-each could reveal a different underlying issue to address.

- Never let anyone tell you what you cannot be. Chase the impossible. Maintain your cool and integrity in the face of adversity and rejection. Cry with your friends who will love and support you. Then pick yourself up, put on your big girl panties and say..."I'll show you". Our life's journey is not always the straight path to your destination. The bumps and even times of rejection give us character and depth.

- A few tips to help you with re-entry into the workforce and your next job in leadership include: 1) Stay current and collect as much information as possible during your time away from the job, 2) Update your resume, 3) Find the right job match that aligns with your interests and passion, 4) Prepare for the interview-anticipate their questions and prepare some of your own for the interview panel, 5) Believe in yourself and abilities.

- Most people who have made it to the ranks of leadership thrive in a work environment that promotes continuous growth and development.

- Having faith in your abilities, reframing the possibilities for your future and being courageous will set the stage for your future success if you are faced with the decision to leave your current job. Other doors will open for you. Fear can blind you to what might be right in front of you.

- It's time to stand up and speak your mind…assertiveness is not a sin! And, if done well and using "respectful truth-telling", you can get the respect that you desire and, many times what you want. For leaders, assertiveness is an essential skill for success.

- It only takes **one** difficult employee to create havoc and discourse in an organization. And, despite your strongest wishes, these problem employees and the ripple affect they have on an organization will not go away. This is not a time for leader passivity. All eyes are upon you as the leader to see how you will handle the situation. Remember, the performance of the difficult employee is not a secret. Everyone is aware and hopes someone does something about them.

- If you choose to ignore or have a slow response to a difficult employee, you could actually escalate an already tense workplace dynamic. Word of mouth spreads quickly, causing problems recruiting fresh talent into the organization or department- no one wants to work with this person. If the employee's behavior impacts work flow and productivity, now it has financial implications attached to it. Further complications can occur when decision making, scheduling or other processes have to be changed to work around the difficult employee. The more critical fallout is that there is a perceived lack of commitment to an organization's standards and work ethic because leadership is tolerating a behavior that is in complete violation of a condition of employment.

- During the meeting with a difficult employee remember to use simple, clear language, give concrete examples, and explain what makes their behavior, attitude or performance a problem. Give the employee a chance to respond, but not to argue. You want to be crystal clear about what improved performance will look like, and then give a reasonable timeframe for it to occur. It's very important to convey that you want the employee to succeed, but you do that best by being clear about what you need. Wrap up the meeting, assuring the employee that there will be both help and follow-up. And please, document, document, document! Set up a file and keep records of all relevant documents and correspondence.

- Community service is and has always been the mark of true leadership- the ability to give back **unconditionally**. It's that steadfast dedication to improving the community in which you work and live for the future and, using your leadership skills to be a positive role model to others. Community service can take many forms: individual mentoring, empowering groups, fund raising, teaching, participating in community projects (i.e., *Habitat for Humanity*) and a variety of other support services. It is a reciprocal proposition, with both parties gaining from the experience.

- In many workplaces there is very little awareness of menopause as a potential health issue; it is a 'taboo' topic. Women are often embarrassed to disclose their problems or fear that their bosses would be embarrassed if they raised the subject, particularly if those they report to are younger than them or male.

- Support for menopausal women can be increased, through more non-judgmental education and awareness, more flexible working hours and, crucial, improvements in work place temperature control and ventilation.

- If you want to start your own business, know the rules of the game: 1) Start with passion, 2) Identify your target audience, 3) Identify your hook, 4) Do your homework, 5) Develop your business plan, 6) Find your first customers, 7) Remain optimistic and realistic.

- At work, generational differences can affect everything, including recruiting, building teams, dealing with change, motivating, managing, and maintaining and increasing productivity. Think of how generational differences, relative to how people communicate, might affect misunderstandings, high employee turnover, difficulty in attracting employees and gaining employee commitment.

- The leadership characteristics favored by women give us a leg up in working across a variety of generations. Leverage those traits for success- people development, setting clear expectations and rewards, role modeling, inspirational leadership, and participative decision making. Men who continue to lead with an approach grounded in control may find themselves at odds with the new aged workforce. And remember ladies, awareness and communication form the base for the secret sauce.

- Because of its many consequences, it's important to deal with burnout right away. This is different than occasional periods of high stress. Stressed people can still imagine that if they can just get everything under control, they'll feel better. The first step in healing burnout is to be able to recognize the symptoms in yourself or have a safe friend or colleague to give you honest feedback. Step two is to stop being victim and change your current state. Look for ways to better manage your stress or seek professional support. Step three is to build up your internal bank account by taking better care of your physical and emotional health. Step four would be if all the previous steps fail…exit stage right! Your well-being is an essential ingredient to being a great leader.

- Be a shero to someone else.

We all have the power to make choices in our lives. Begin to make some choices that put you first! Take back your life! Remember, there is no magic pill and each person's journey to a balanced life is personal. However, there are numerous approaches or strategies you can try… the first step is realizing you are out of balance. Running is not healthy and should not be the norm. As mothers to future women leaders, we need to continue to offer our daughters the foundation and inner strength for success. It is a precious gift. They need to hold their own and wear a yellow suit!

References:

AARP Bulletin (January-February, 2010, page 47)

ABOUT THE AUTHOR

Jackie is a high performing Senior Executive with a progressive career encompassing more than 30 years of sustained leadership and accomplishments with major health systems and organizations. With passion, creative energy and vision, she motivates diverse groups of people toward success. She has dedicated most of her career to the advancement of quality health care programs throughout the United States, particularly those focused on the care of the poor and underserved. She has worked in a variety of roles, starting her career as a nurse working for Johns Hopkins Health Institutions, including management, health education, and program coordination. Upon graduation from her master's program she went to work for Health Care for the Homeless, Inc. in Baltimore, Maryland as a Nurse Practitioner serving over 50,000 vulnerable patients per year in clinics, shelters and the streets. In 1987, she was appointed as its first President & CEO and developed this organization into a national model.

In 1999, Jackie was appointed Vice President of Community Health Systems Integration for Bon Secours Baltimore Health System. There Jackie led an effective $15 million turn-around initiative called Transformation 2000. In 2000 Jackie joined the Providence Health System in Oregon, as Chief Executive for Providence Milwaukee Hospital and Regional Chief Executive for Ancillary Business. While at Providence, Jackie took Providence Milwaukee to Top 100 Hospital in the U.S. three times and implemented the organization's Family Practice Residency Program. In 2007 Jackie left Providence to become the President and CEO of Mercy Health Partners for Northeast Pennsylvania, where she had oversight for two hospitals and 15 other freestanding clinics and diagnostic centers.

Jackie lectures all over the country and has received numerous awards along the way. She has written and published her first book, "Believing You Can Fly" which offers insight to her career journey in an attempt to inspire others to pursue their dreams against what may seem to be insurmountable odds. Today, Jackie is an Executive Coach for Studer Group. She lives in North Carolina with her husband Wesley, enjoying the beauty and rich culture of the area.

It is with great love and deep respect that I dedicate this book to my #1 shero, my mom, Goldie Keyes. Your love and support gave me the will and strength for my life's journey. I will forever be grateful. You showed me what being a shero was all about. I love you Mom.
—Jackie

THE LAST WORD

Dearest Jackie,

I constantly think of you with much love. I often run over in my mind the beginning-from the time when you were born I watched you continue to grow year by year and now in my eyes you are you the great lady that I knew that you would become. Jackie you bring me many happy moments to live through. We have a connection that helps to shape both of our lives in a wonderful way, and we have a bond that through life's ups and downs it will always be there, it is a family tie that has grown in our lives, a gift that continues to grow in our heart. It is a gift from God, and may God continue to bless you my daughter.

Lots of love,
Ma

CPSIA information can be obtained
at www.ICGtesting.com
Printed in the USA
FSOW03n0007130217
30656FS